JOURNEY OF A LIFETIME
By Richard Askew

ISBN: 978-1-873061-04-6
First published 2015
Copyright © Richard Askew
Printed by GH Cityprint, 58-60 Middlesex Street, London E1 7EZ
Published by CHARISMA BOOKS, www.johnwrites.co
Design and publishing services: Nicholas Spencer, emailnickles@gmail.com

*Dedicated to my wife, Margaret,
my companion on the way*

After payment of costs, from each book sold, £1 will go to Juba Diocesan Model Secondary School in South Sudan, to help pay for a student who would otherwise not be able to afford the fees.
A further £1 will go to Bath Abbey's major 'Footprint Project'; designed to equip the Abbey further to proclaim the faith for the future.

Contents

Foreword

The writer AW Tozer once offered the thought "let us practice the fine art of making every work a priestly ministration. Let us believe that God is in all our simple deeds and learn to find Him there". That, for me, sums up this excellent and marvellous book. I can't think of a similar book that so simply, clearly and humorously offers an appraisal of Christian service in terms that everyone can relate to.

My links with Richard and Margaret Askew began when I was Bishop of Bath and Wells in the late 1980s. The historic church of Bath Abbey was seeking a new rector. Richard recounts the story of a few senior lay people in Bath Abbey who, initially, resisted his appointment. I was frustrated by the opposition they raised and, under the rules of the time, I appealed to the Archbishop of Canterbury to allow Richard an opportunity to meet the Abbey Church Council. This was done and, as I expected, Richard's personality and vision won the day and he became an outstanding rector of that historic place.

But this is to enter the story half way through. Richard's book is a personal and moving account of a pilgrimage that began before the Second World War and which weaves its way through an immensely interesting life. I found in this narrative many parallels with my own journey: the terrifying impact of the war, service in the military, university education, the call of ordination, the meeting of one's life partner and the gift of children. Throughout this absorbing story there is no missing the influence of Margaret's support and their love for one another.

The story is told with lovely touches of humour and humility. Richard is a great observer of human nature and his comments, never at any point malicious, had me rocking with laughter.

Nevertheless, he makes no secret of hardship in the ministry, to which I and my wife can easily identify. The ordained ministry is not for the faint-hearted. Those who seek in it a career like any other are surely going to miss the glory of it, because it cannot be assessed in terms of financial or social reward only in terms of serving Christ and expressing it in devoted service.

Of course, we have to acknowledge that Richard's story is not a very common one in terms of the ordained ministry. After all, it is not everyone who gets to become Canon of Salisbury Cathedral and ends up as Rector of Bath Abbey! But, by some token, it is not everyone who can sit lightly to privilege and serve so selflessly.

Reading this book was for me a real delight and I commend it wholeheartedly.

GEORGE CAREY
Lord Carey was Archbishop of Canterbury, 1991-2002

Point of departure

The ambulance reversed neatly down the drive to our front door at 8.00am, just six minutes after Margaret's telephone call. The angina attack had been sharp – not a warning to ignore. In no time at all I was carried downstairs by two cheery paramedics and we were running smoothly on our way to Bath's Royal United Hospital.

Sunday morning seemed to be a good time to enter hospital and the A&E team had got to work right away on an exhaustive series of tests. They rapidly chewed over the results and spat me out into the assessment ward. And that is where I came to rest.

It was then that I began to see a long, long wait stretching before me – days, certainly, and possibly weeks. How to fill the time? Why not advance the plan I had formed some time beforehand – to set down my memories of 69 years of full and joyful living? I hastened to reassure myself that this was not because of the possibility of a permanent guillotine being dropped across my endeavours but simply as a useful way of using this unexpected bonus of enforced idleness.

Such an exercise, of course, is often derided as the last infirmity of ignoble minds, a final starburst of egotism. Yet, at the same time, we all share a common fund of experience and one person's story touches us all. Just possibly the story I have to tell might resonate with others. Besides this, we each have a natural curiosity to discover whether or not our path through life betrays any sign of purpose and direction, or whether we have simply been engaged in pottering around aimlessly, letting life happen to us. Only by setting out one's memories can we detect any sort of underlying pattern.

One hot afternoon many years ago, I found myself standing on the banks of the River Nile, up on a low mud cliff, contemplating a scene of great animation below. Pulled in to the shore was a spanking new ferryboat. The ramp was down and passengers were streaming on board. First went the cattle; then the women, encumbered with large water-pots on their heads and every sort of baggage in their arms; finally the men strolled on board, empty-handed apart from the odd walking stick, talking loftily to each other about matters of great importance. Finally, the boat was full, the ramp went up and they cast off. Then a curious thing happened. Rather than heading across the wide river to the far bank, the boat turned upstream and executed a mighty circle before returning to its course. This was too much for my curiosity and I questioned a local about it. "Oh," he said, "in the old days, when we had the good old British ferryboat, it went nice and slowly and there was plenty of time to sell the tickets. Now, with the new American boat, it goes much too fast, so we have to make more time."

I have sometimes been tempted to ask myself whether I was heading in a definite direction, or whether I was simply going round and round in wider and wider circles. Hopefully the following pages will provide an answer to my question.

RICHARD ASKEW

Chapter 1

LOST WORLD

One of life's little landmarks has to be our very first act of sheer, pure wickedness. I well recall my first-ever sin: it was dastardly indeed. It must have been around Easter, probably 1938, and my brother, Brian (a superior being with eight years to my two), had been given a large chocolate rabbit, complete with bobtail. I deeply coveted that rabbit and took the first opportunity to seek it out: to eat it all would have been risky, asking for detection, so I contented myself by biting off the tail alone. It was every bit as good as it looked. I concealed the crime by nibbling off the edges so neatly that it looked as if the rabbit had always been tail-less. Quite unaware of cheeks daubed with chocolate stains, I faced my mother brightly when she discovered me. "Did you bite off the tail?" she demanded, for she had not been fooled by my damage limitation. I looked her in the eye and without hesitation answered "Not me!" She took it as a great joke; yet my sense of guilt has survived the intervening 67 years.

However, conflict with the moral law played a very small part in my childhood. We all have a problem distinguishing what we remember from what we have been told we ought to remember. My first few years basked in the palmy days of peace – albeit an increasingly fragile peace. Naturally, the sun always shone, especially on our annual summer holidays, usually spent in a rented cottage at West Wittering on the Sussex coast. Only a track separated us from the shoreline. The sable sands squelched serenely for miles to right and left. Our beach toys were made of tin or of wood, as it was years before the plastic revolution was to hit the toy industry. Walls' 'Stop Me And Buy One' men peddled busily along the beach road, their tricycles propelling a massive freeze-box full of ice-creams. On one magic day we drove westwards to Southampton Water to watch spellbound as the Queen Mary put to sea.

It was almost as sunny back home. We lived in a quiet suburban road that lived up to its name, Woodlands Way, in Carshalton, Surrey. My father was a partner in an old-established corn and seed business in East Grinstead. In this capacity he had to travel once a week up to London to buy stock through the Corn Exchange: his other days were spent at the firm in Sussex. It thus suited him well to live half-way between the two: at least, it did as long as we were at peace.

Our house was detached, with a long lawn stretching behind it to a wire fence, beyond which stretched mysterious and menacing woodland. Bushes and a large tree, ideal for climbing, marked the end of our domain. My father dug out a goldfish pond half way from the house, into which I duly fell on several occasions, nearly nipping this narrative in the bud. Nearby a walnut tree carpeted the ground with delicious nuts as well as providing a home for red squirrels. Altogether

Self and father

4

it provided a paradise for two small boys with bikes. An Irish maid completed the ménage, no unusual thing then for a middle-class family such as ours.

One historic memory juts up above the plain of day-to-day living. In 1939 I was taken in my pushchair down to the nearest shopping centre, in Sutton. We entered a large electrical store, where we joined an excited circle of shoppers. Then – wonder of wonders! – we were treated to the first-ever televised Derby. No matter that the screen was tiny, the black-and-white image flickery, and Epsom itself only a couple of miles down the road: it was still a technological miracle. Shortly afterwards TV was to be closed down and to go underground 'for the duration'. Nevertheless, the IT revolution had taken a great leap forward.

On the home front, I achieved distinction by painting myself all over with oil paint, a sort of walking rainbow, and then, appalled, hiding in bed to escape detection: my sheets were multi-coloured for long afterwards. Then there was the day of appalling stomach-pain, which led to a speedy operation for acute appendicitis. My subsequent recuperation took weeks, in sharp contrast to the couple of days in hospital required for today's keyhole surgery. Finally, there was the exciting evening when my father set out to cut through an electric lead that he thought was not plugged in. The resultant flash and bang were sensational and left him holding only a bone handle: the knife had melted. It was a good precursor to the flashes and bangs that were shortly to ensue.

For a shadow was creeping up on our sunlit existence. Over the relative tranquillity of home life the international scene was darkening. Even as a four-year-old I could pick up the vibes of anxiety sparking between the grown-ups. Recalcitrant children a century and a half before had been threatened with 'Boney'; for us the convenient bogeyman to hustle us off to bed was 'Musso' or 'Adolf'.

My father had served throughout the First World War: indeed it could be said to have been the defining event of his life, lifting him out of his job as junior clerk in the City of London and dragging him through the trenches of France and a sideshow war in Salonica, on to an eventual commission in the Surrey Yeomanry. The circumstances of this promotion are revealing. Officer casualties had been so high that it was no longer possible to recruit more from the traditional reservoir of 'gentlemen'. Accordingly, it was discreetly conceded at the very highest levels in the War Office that, as my father would tell us with glee, a new category of 'temporary gentlemen' should be recognised. Hence his posting from the steamy heat of Salonica to the cool of the cavalry officers training school at the Curragh, in what is now The Republic of Ireland. Here the threat to be faced came not from the continent but nearer home, from local Irish nationalists.

Though the war was the time my father had lived most intensely (as well as providing him with a repertoire of much-repeated stories), it had left him, along with a dread of war's destructive horror, with a deep distrust of the Germans. A trickle-down effect imbued me with the same attitude, not to be budged until 1992 (just hang in there, gentle reader).

Early in 1939 my father, streets ahead of many self-deceived politicians, took a prescient step. Builders arrived and, to my amazement, knocked out the back wall of the pantry. They then proceeded to build on a large square room, with walls and roof a foot thick. It had one window aperture, secured not with glass but with a thick steel shutter. It was in fact a customised, one-off air raid shelter, in which subsequently the whole family was to spend its nights. Things were getting serious.

We were on holiday at our beloved Wittering on the August day when war finally came. That day I sensed that all the grown-ups had suddenly grown very serious. They gathered around a large wood-encased wireless set, from which came the lugubrious tones of Prime Minister Neville Chamberlain's defeated voice. "I have to tell you that no such undertaking has been received from Herr Hitler… We are accordingly in a state of war with Germany."

Action followed rapidly on the heels of words. An old man on a decrepit bicycle came pedalling down the track separating the cottage from the beach. He was vigorously ringing a hand bell and turned out to be the best that could be managed at the time in the way of an air

6

raid warning. Much shaken by this apocalyptic forerunner, we bundled out of the house and made for the nearest ditch. Crouching in its muddy bottom, we gazed up at a startling scene unfolding above us. High up against the blue of a perfect summer day we could see a little silver biplane pottering across the sky. Below it, smoky puff-balls were languidly unfolding themselves. It transpired that a private pilot of defective imagination had decided on this of all days to enjoy a last, leisurely, peacetime spin out across the Channel. He had flown out in peacetime but returned to find us at war. He was apparently totally unaware that he was likely to arouse the fury of the ack-ack (anti-aircraft artillery) guns. Needless to say, the shells were bursting far short of their target and no damage was done. The terrified pilot eventually made it back to his landing strip – no doubt the better for a sharp lesson in political awareness.

Pre-war was over.

Chapter 2

WAR THROUGH THE NURSERY WINDOW

I was four when war broke out and 10 when it finished. It therefore dominated my childhood, seized my imagination, shaped what we could and could not do, and was a constant source of routine-breaking excitement. Apart from an initial period in Carshalton, I was fortunate to be living for most of it out in the Sussex countryside, sheltered from the nightmare of incessant air raids. The horror was usually hidden. The immediate consequence of the outbreak of war from my point of view was that all the grown-ups immediately became chronically irritable. I now see what a burden of anxiety they carried. Serious attack from the air was a new reality, not previously experienced: the only pointers were the horror stories that had come out of Spain. Would Carshalton become another Guernica in a few weeks? Would the Germans use poison gas, as they had in the previous conflict? Confidence was not increased by having to cram screaming children into horror-film gas-masks. Yes, I can understand why the grown-ups were on a short fuse. Even my dear mother's customarily placid and serene temperament was badly shaken.

Patriotism – or panic – produced a tremendous response to the appeal to hand in aluminium cooking pots to make Spitfires, those charismatic aircraft on which, along with the Hurricane, our hopes for air defence rested. Our propaganda media turned up their inane optimism full blast. They rightly lauded "the Few", in Winston Churchill's words, who flew these planes: undisclosed was the high-octane aviation fuel secretly imported from the United States that gave them their edge in speed and climb. In time these heroes tipped the balance and gained superiority in the Battle of Britain. From the vantage point of my father's shoulders one day I watched a distant sky-scape of dogfights. That was the occasion when the radio trumpeted that 100 German planes had been shot down in one day. In fact, it turned out in time that the real number was closer to 70 but it was enough: supremacy had been achieved.

From a five-year-old viewpoint it must be admitted that all this was rather exciting. Collecting our sanitised cigarette cards, we struggled to complete our series of Great British Generals. We bellowed out *We'll Hang Out the Washing on the Siegfried Line* and other such hopeful lyrics. Three events injected some reality into our view of the war. First, we rapidly got used to the sight of wounded soldiers in their blue uniforms strolling out from the nearby military hospital. Then exaggerated fears of the threat of paratroop landings led to the burning off of Carshalton Common, a fearsome portent for a small boy: the only casualties were hundreds of scorched rabbits. Finally, the long-threatened bombing came closer; although we were far from the heart of London, isolated night-time bombs from fleeing bombers became frequent occurrences. We accordingly moved into our domestic blockhouse and slept there each night in tolerable comfort on mattresses on the floor. It was a great thing to fling open the metal shutter on to a lovely sunny morning, to the sound of the wailing 'All Clear'. The 'All Clear' note was good to hear but anything like the 'Alert' still makes my stomach churn.

One aspect of the war had an immediate effect on our family circumstances. The government closed down the Corn Exchange in London and organised corn distribution by direct, centralised allocation. There was, therefore, not much point in staying on in Carshalton as a sitting target for windy German bomber pilots lightening their loads above us. The logical thing was to move to where the business was located – East Grinstead, due south in Sussex.

Our new home was a substantial house called Hillside, looking down on to a crossroads and facing on the opposite hill to the south of us a sunken road between rocky walls. Unfortunately for my parents, in the panic gripping the country after the retreat from Dunkirk in 1940, the Home Guard identified our home as the ideal site for 'Custer's Last Stand', when the expected invaders flooded up from the coast 25 miles away. With great enthusiasm they dug foxholes and weapon pits across the garden and on one wonderful day actually set up a trench mortar and sent a few practise rounds flying over the crossroads into the field behind. Their efforts were directed with great enthusiasm by an elderly Boer War general, deaf as a post, who had taken a dip in rank to run our local 'Dad's Army'. I have no doubt the war gave him a fresh lease of life.

After the Home Guard came the Canadians, the only fully equipped units in the South of England at that dire moment in our national affairs. The Canadians surrounded the garden with a barbed wire entanglement and taught me to sing *Gentille Allouette*. By now our home was an impregnable fortress, capable of resisting any onslaught. A German tank rash enough to advance down the sunken road would be knocked out by the setting off of an explosive charge in the barrels of oil embedded in the rock walls. Any survivors would be immediately wiped out by one or two well directed mortar rounds from the Home Guard.

Meanwhile my father was flinging his weight behind the war effort. A local committee, representing the emergency services and volunteers, was formed to lay plans for enemy attack and invasion. The human mind, when confronted with a situation too large to comprehend, tends to take refuge in the comfortingly trivial: if the big picture is too complex for us to grasp, we can at least arrange our pens and pencils tidily. So it was that the committee, faced with the prospect of bombed-out households, solemnly decided that a neat parcel of 10 bricks should be delivered to each home to build a field cooker in the brick-strewn ruins of their property. The wherewithal for bread making was also to be stockpiled. At this point the police superintendent, hitherto silent, saw his chance to make a decisive intervention in the discussion: "What are you planning to do," he demanded, "about jam?".

More seriously, my father joined the Guinea Pig Club. The club was the brainchild of the New Zealander Sir Archibald McIndoe, the pioneering plastic surgeon, at East Grinstead's Queen Victoria Hospital. It was to enable burnt airmen, patched up by McIndoe's unit, to recover their confidence through meeting locals socially. So my father's role was to be on parade at 11.00am daily in a local hostelry to buy drinks for pilots whose horrible facial wounds had been treated with primitive skin grafts. There was a battle to be won in enabling them to overcome their fears and to re-enter normal society.

Until 1943, apart from our frenzied preparations, the war largely left us alone. As I have hinted, such disruption as there was for me amounted to – let's face it – excitement. This was, of course, not the view of my parents: I remember their expressions as they stood by the shed where I used to play and prized a stray machine-gun bullet out of the woodwork, a reminder of aerial combat overhead.

One day in 1943, however, the full horror came to our little country town. In the early afternoon a German bomber, pursued by a couple of Spitfires, burst out of the cloud. The pilot, seeing a town below, jettisoned his bombs. They hit the cinema, where a children's matinee was showing, and collapsed the roof on the audience below. Over 100 died in the blast and ensuing fire. On my way home from school I looked in horror at the flames belching out of the façade of a familiar building. I was gazing at the reality of the blitz, which had become a nightly experience in London and other big cities.

One other isolated bombing raid in the town centre brought the reality of war close to us, although on this occasion there were few killed. Everyone from the community who was available, my father among them, rushed to dig out the casualties from the ruins. When they had been toiling away at this macabre task for an hour or so, they became aware of big black Rolls Royce that had drawn up behind them. It was King George VI, who happened to be in the area and had been informed of the raid. Some of the rescue workers were brought up to be presented to him. My father's immediate feeling was one of alarm at the deplorable state of his soot and dust-stained clothing; not fit for a king.

Over the next year a fresh and terrible weapon was launched at us, the V1, or 'doodlebug', as we tried to normalise it, was a small pilotless jet plane carrying, nevertheless, a massive punch of high explosive. Launched from numerous sites in the Pas de Calais at hourly intervals, doodlebugs converged on London, passing over

Sussex and Kent on the way. The noise of their passage was terrifying but not nearly as bad as the explosion that followed when the engine cut out. As long as you could hear the engine you were safe. Their Achilles heel was that they flew relatively slow and straight, providing a good target for guns and fighters. The capital was protected by a forest of barrage balloons on an east-west line north of Croydon. The task, therefore, was to shoot them down south of that line. The fighters were warned off, when they got near the balloon lines, by parachute flares fired by army detachments positioned in a further line near us. For us boys this provided some thrilling moments dashing across the fields to be the first to collect a silk parachute from the ground. They were highly esteemed trophies.

Our school sat on a plateau alongside a deep valley. We were all gathered in the school hall one afternoon for weekly 'Marks', a ritual when the headmaster, an awe-inspiring descendant of the 19th century Prime Minister William Gladstone, would summon us out to the mark board, row by row, where, in ringing tones, he would excoriate the idle and hold up the virtuous for imitation. Suddenly the dreaded roar indicated a doodlebug flying up the valley, almost on a level with the tall windows of the hall. The snort of the engine was joined by the rat-tat of a Spitfire's machine guns. My row had just been summoned across the room and was gathered by the marks board. Nobody moved. Suddenly an almighty detonation showed the fighter had hit the right spot. Immediately some of the windows fell in. Fortunately no one was hurt but on my seat, when I returned to it, were foot-long shards of razor-sharp glass.

It was only the invasion of the Continent, in June 1944, that terminated these attacks, as the launch pads were progressively over-run. Living where we were, it was impossible to be unaware of the preparations for that mighty undertaking. Every tree in Ashdown Forest appeared to conceal a truck, gun or tank. From their points of concealment in every scrap of southern woodland, troops were waiting to stream down to the coast and their points of embarkation. It was at this time in the war that the number of US forces reached parity with British, Canadian and other Commonwealth forces. Such was the weight of manpower gathered and waiting that the man in charge of the whole invasion, General Dwight D Eisenhower, commented that the only thing stopping the south-east sinking under the sea was the massive number of barrage balloons holding it all up! When D-Day finally arrived, the relief and jubilation were intense. I have a vivid memory of watching, on my way to school, a sky patterned from horizon to horizon with massive gliders and their tow-planes on their way for the initial attack.

The location of the target beaches for the invasion was the world's best-kept secret. A ludicrous leak provided a small hole in the overall security blanket. A housemaster at Leatherhead School had a sideline occupation making up crosswords for one of the daily newspapers. Under pressure of time he set some boys in detention the task of constructing the last few clues. Unfortunately for him, the answers they chose were words picked up by the boys in their chats with American troops camped in the nearby woodland. The appearance in the puzzle of 'Overlord', code-name of the whole invasion, prompted a rapid visit from MI5 and lengthy explanations.

As this massive and irresistible onslaught got under way, we avidly followed progress in the newspaper maps. Soon French and American troops were on the road for Paris. By this time we had a lodger – an elderly French refugee called Mademoiselle Schaeffer, along with a malodorous little dog, Togo. On the day that Paris fell, we heard a terrible crashing from her room above our heads accompanied by feverish barking from Togo: Mlle. Schaeffer was prancing round in a dance of victory. She was right to do so, even though it was to be another year yet before peace finally came.

Chapter 3

SHAM PEARLS BEFORE REAL SWINE

This classic definition of the educational venture would certainly have fitted the first serious school I attended, at least with regard to the product on offer and probably the porcine qualities of its recipients. At the Abbey School, Ashurst Wood, both syllabus and teaching method could kindly be described as conservative. Latin was a staple, followed by French – for parsing and translating, of course, and never for speaking. English poetry was for learning (good, that); lesson in German were seen as unpatriotic and not taught. Everything had to be analysed and memorised but not necessarily investigated and understood. A fair grounding, at any rate.

The school, housed in an old country house, was set in beautiful grounds, looking out over Forest Row to Ashdown Forest beyond. There were trees to climb, bushes to hide in with one's gang, pinecones to throw, and conkers to do battle with.

All of this did much to compensate for the school's gastronomic nightmares and the bizarre eccentricities of the teaching staff. Corned beef was the best bet at lunch, preferable to whale meat and snoek and a variety of other unspeakable fish dredged up from the profound depths of the Atlantic. School food everywhere was to remain abysmal up to the 1950s.

At the time when I joined the school, in 1943, the only staff who could be recruited were a job lot of ladies of uncertain temper; dug-out First World War officers; and stringy young men exempted from the call-up. The ex-officers were the best bet: what they lacked in academic knowledge they made up for in sheer grip. One of the stringy young men borrowed an advance from the headmaster of £20 – a vast sum – to start a Scout troop but was then no more seen. Another, a very soulful young man with Bing Crosby eyes and a great gift for teaching scripture, ended up in Lewes jail for some unspeakable crime.

Over this array of mediocre talent presided not one but two headmasters, occasionally at odds to our great delight. They put on a speech day at the end of each of the three terms, two for internal consumption only, one in the summer to impress the parents. Parents are, of course, a perpetual source of embarrassment to chaps at school. It was, therefore, a terrible day when, not having learnt the system, I told my mother to attend one of the parentless internal speech days. She was, nevertheless, courteously received by the headmaster, who seated her up on the platform with the staff. I kept my eyes rigidly down on the floor until my neighbour jogged me and said aggressively: "Who's that woman?" "I don't know," I answered – and the cock crowed.

Despite its shortcomings, the school survived until the 1960s. Shortly before its closure a friend of mine from my time at Oxford University got a temporary post teaching there. On his second day a senior master approached him in the common room. "Have you read *Decline And Fall*?" he enquired. My friend had not. "You should", said the master, "if you want to understand this place."

Nevertheless, there must have been academic gold among the dross of the teaching. I was eventually twitched up to such a pitch that it was deemed safe to enter me for a scholarship for Harrow "for the experience". I can still remember the insulting expression of amazement on the face of the headmaster when he advanced on me with a telegram telling me I had been successful.

Meanwhile, there had been a major development on the home front. Towards the end of the war the London County Council wanted a large house in the country where expectant mums could be housed in peace for the last months of their pregnancies, away from the bombing. They selected 'The Knapp', a 1900 house on a quiet road outside East Grinstead. It had numerous rooms, an acre of garden with a tennis court and, behind it, a small lake. Ideal. They did it up, regardless of expense, and even put down linoleum in the kitchen, an unbelievable luxury. It was all completed just one week before the first doodlebug puttered overhead: The Knapp proved to be sited just under one of their regular routes. Useless for its intended purpose, the house lay empty until 1947, when it was put up for sale, heavily discounted. My father, with his accustomed acumen, got in quick and bought it. The family fortunes had risen to a new plateau and we two boys had a wonderful home in which to grow up.

The exceptionally bitter winter of 1947, however, concealed our good fortune from us. For a country anyway on its knees economically with many dire shortages, the bitter cold and the disruption of the transport was a very severe blow, causing real hardship. In our new house we were snowed in for days and my father was to be seen, drip on nose and with a coal bucket in each hand, constantly bustling, bent double, from one coal fire to the next.

The Knapp stood a considerable way from the Abbey School. Normally a couple of buses got me there but if something went wrong I not infrequently walked the whole way, six miles, only to be scolded on arrival for being late. What would happen today?

This journey, however, was not required of me for very long. In the autumn of 1948 I was taken off, with a heavy and anxious heart, to begin my first term at Harrow. One of the school songs runs *'How the buttons on his blue coat shone / How he sang and he carolled like a bird! / He went off to Harrow, tra la la / And was placed in the Lower, Lower Third'*. For me, singing and carolling were definitely not on the agenda. I was entering a new and terrifying world, to which I was not at all sure I belonged. Financially, my going to Harrow was going to mean a considerable sacrifice for my father, even with the help of the scholarship. Socially – the most important factor in those class-ridden days – this was to mean a new and rarefied world to which we did not belong. We were punching above our weight.

The reality was both better and worse than my expectations. Life at the school was by any standards Spartan. The food, as everywhere, was grim. Butter and sugar were still rationed and there was free market trading with our weekly saucer of butter and half jam-jar of sugar. Restrictions on heating fuel meant that, after rugby, every six-inch-deep bathful of warm water had to be used five times; the last occupant merely redistributing the mud. We lived in two-boy bed-sits, each one heated, incredibly, by its own coal fire. Every other morning we would troop down to the basement to collect our bucket of coal and packet of kindling. The fire risk must have been high and, indeed, one governor had the reputation of having once burnt down his own school house.

Discipline was, putting it mildly, firm. During the war pupil numbers had shrunk, as parents were unwilling to locate their sons too close to London's bombing. Consequently, an 'open-door' policy was pursued as soon as peace came to replenish the school up to the requisite 550-600, spread over 11 residential houses. Unfortunately, this led to the admission of a core of undesirables. By 1948 these hard-liners were being as assiduously purged as any Communist regime could have wished. Proximity to London presented the temptation to nip down to the Underground station and have a night on the town. Stories were told of inebriated lines of revellers parading, arms linked, down the High Street at 3am, singing lustily. However, a new broom headmaster was dealing firmly with the situation.

At house level, discipline was maintained by a rigid hierarchy of privilege. At the summit was the Housemaster, abetted by the House Matron. Below him stood a senior boy – but nevertheless a god-like figure – the Head of House, supported by two or three House Monitors. They had individual studies and the services of numerous 'fags' (near slaves, who for a year or two fulfilled a number of petty duties). Next in order were the Three-yearers, invested with useful privileges such as being able to rest their behinds on the tepid corridor radiators. Two-yearers had their feet on the bottom rung of this *cursus honorum* with one or two paltry dress privileges tossed to them. At the bottom of the stack were the wretched first year fags, either apportioned individually to one of the Monitors or in a pool answerable to a 'call'; any Monitor could step into the corridor and issue an eldritch wolf-call: "Boy! Boy! Booooy!". Pandemonium ensued as every available fag raced to him from all over the house. The last to arrive had to take the letter to the post, or whatever the errand was. "Lying doggo" to escape this servitude was a serious offence, punishable by beating.

Beating was, in fact, the mainstay sanction of the hierarchy. It was administered either by the Head of House or, in more serious cases, by the Housemaster. 'Executions' by the Head of House took place three or four times a term and were attended with considerable ritual. They took place immediately after Lights Out in the House Library. Silence would fall over the whole establishment – the silence that must enfold Death Row – until a single Boy! call would produce the duty fag. His task was to summon the accused to the place of execution. Justice was satisfied by a short homily followed by four strokes of the cane. Only once was I on the receiving end and that was a miscarriage of justice.

Moment of glory

A lesser buttress to the system was achieved by a meticulous dress code that suppressed us under straw hats and put us, on Sundays, into tailcoats and wing collars. Sunday wear for the great and the good was a top hat, gleaming with Brylcream. Again, time in the school opened up a graded procession of privileges; brown shoes, for instance, were achieved in the third year. The only thing that made the whole system tolerable was the thought that one day you too would aspire to the peak of the pyramid. During the 1960s a satirical film, *If*, was produced, planned as a black caricature of the worst aspects of public school life: much of its impact was lost on me, since many of its features seemed to me perfectly familiar and not grossly overstated, if at all.

Like all schools, Harrow was dedicated to maximising achievement as a preparation for doing the same in life-after-school. One of the songs envisaged the school as a 'treeful of monkeys' and ended triumphantly *'There wasn't a doubt that nine out of ten / Would be found at the top of the tree.'* Avenues of achievement were, however, somewhat limited in those austere days. It was sport, sport, sport (a different major sport each term), with academic, musical and other creative achievement coming a poor third after minor sports. The Philathletic Club provided a shop-window – and the fanciest waistcoats – for the top sportsmen. Watching school matches was compulsory, on pain of beating – a requirement that has put me off watching most sport for ever after. I was a poor sportsman; having achieved my height of 6ft 1.5ins at age 14. I was poorly co-ordinated. I had no music. The prospect was dim.

As a soft option for cricket, which bored me, I took up long-range shooting and would bus off weekly to Bisley for hours on the ranges. Here, to my surprise, I found myself in the company of two Middle Eastern princes – Hussein of Jordan and Feisal of Iraq. They no doubt saw rifle shooting more in the light of vocational training than sport. It did poor Feisal little good: he and his family were assassinated.

So far I have stressed the downside of what was a highly privileged path. What were the plus points? Close pastoral care and the inspiration of some fine minds. Our housemaster, George McConnell, limited by shyness from easy relationships with parents, gave himself unstintingly to knowing and encouraging boys in his care. Every evening he would prowl the house, dropping in to chat with half a dozen boys in their rooms. Later on he would keep open house in his study to Monitors, who could drop in and demand beer.

The same personal attention was evident with the teaching staff. Our form-master took us all to the school library before the summer holidays and individually married us up with a book. Mine was *Anna Karenina* and I was enthralled by a novel I would never have chosen by myself. Another master once produced this half-term report on me, for my housemaster's eyes only: "Askew has had a fair term so far and any slight criticisms I might have had to offer have been drowned by the shouts of acclaim with which he has greeted his own efforts." There was care, wit and stimulation in abundance lavished upon us.

The headmaster, Ralph Moore, was an inspiring figure. He had previously been headmaster of Bristol Grammar School and his move to Harrow was in those days almost unique in crossing the gulf separating state schools from independent schools. I was fortunate to have him as my form-master in the sixth form; a deeply committed Christian, he shared with us more than his scholarship. His nickname was, inevitably, 'Holy Joe'. He organised the school's first ever chest X-ray and felt it his duty to pass through it himself. The only problem uncovered in the whole school population was with himself: he had lung cancer and in due course died from it.

Apart from the inspiration provided by those within the school, there was too the inspiration provided from outside by the various distinguished Old Harrovians, who were invited to speak to us from time to time. Most notable of all these was the Prime Minister himself, Sir Winston Churchill, then in his final term of office. He would come faithfully each autumn to attend a concert of the school songs – a collection of rousing ditties dating from Victorian times and frequently Victorian in sentiment – and sentimentality. Churchill loved them. He would weep copiously as the concert proceeded but always managed some words at the end to stimulate and challenge us.

Four events lit up my senior years. First, the master in charge of the school's weekly broadsheet, *The Harrovian*, asked me out of the blue to join the editorial group. We met on a weekday evening over cocoa and even, occasionally, chocolate biscuits. The experience of learning to write in a disciplined way was valuable but not nearly so precious as the boost given to my morale by being talent-spotted. The school had three clergymen on the staff – one High, one Low and one unfrocked – so that all points of view were represented. Our editor was the unfrocked cleric, (though his 'fault' was simply that of marriage breakdown). He was a man of warmth and wit, and a Rabelaisian turn of humour. He ran a tight news-sheet that contrived to be lively while eschewing sensationalism. In the first edition at the start of a new school year, the list of *personalia* on the front page detailed all the varied sporting achievements of the summer; one year, halfway down the column of matches won and centuries achieved, a modest entry read simply: "Two old boys were crowned during the holidays". They were our Middle Eastern princes. Cool.

The second happening was an invitation to join our housemaster, another boy and an Old Harrovian, now a naval cadet, for a cruise in his yacht round the Solent during the summer holidays. We went aboard the Mosquito at Itchenor, on Chichester Harbour. A 40ft sailing cruiser, she had been 'liberated' from the Germans by the Navy and sold off. Disaster dogged us from the start. A problem with the rigging delayed departure and got us to our berth in Lymington at half-tide; but was it coming in or going out? We misread the tide table and assumed it was going out, which would have laid us flat in the mud. Much effort was spent trying to wedge a baulk of timber against the boat's side to support us, until finally our mistake was discovered when we floated off yet again.

By now we had prevailed on George not to confine our nautical skills to the Solent but to let us nip across to France. The weather looked propitious, the charts were consulted and at midday we said goodbye to the Needles, on the Isle of Wight, and set sail for Cherbourg. Contrary to expectations, however, the wind got up to the strength of a minor gale. Well reefed down, we sped on. The navigation was immaculate, the timing six hours early. Instead of a dawn arrival, we closed on the port's lights at about 11pm. Cherbourg has an outer sea wall, a mile or so out from the inner harbour. At that stage it had been blown up by the Germans and left as a tangled mass of concrete blocks. I was sent forward to the bow to stock the anchor while the seasoned sailors aft scanned the horizon for the red and green lights marking the harbour entrance. Up in the bows I looked up to see, to my amazement, the harbour wall just a couple of hundred yards away, rushing towards us. Of the harbour entrance itself there was no sign. I thought this worth mentioning to the navigators in the stern. We went about double quick but it was too late; our keel had grounded on the concrete blocks of the sea wall. We were stuck fast on what sailors call a lee shore, being slammed sideways against the concrete with every wave. We hastily collected valuables from the cabin, already knee deep with chill water and then, choosing our moment, leapt on to the wall. We had one intact asset, a 6ft wooden dinghy that could take two of us ashore. The naval cadet (who, in true Nelson tradition, had up to this point been paralysed by sea-sickness) and I as an alleged French speaker, were dispatched.

Eventually we reached the inner harbour, we climbed the steps up the wall and set off, dripping sea-weed from our life jackets, into the port. It was near midnight on a warm September Saturday night, the pavement cafés were packed as we squelched towards them, yet we might have been totally invisible: nobody paid the slightest attention to our soggy approach. In the end I found a nautical-looking character, tapped him on the shoulder and said: *"Pardon, monsieur, nous sommes naufragés."* ("Excuse me, sir, we are shipwrecked") . Things then happened rapidly. Our colleagues were rescued and we were lodged in a dry shed for the night. Next morning the pilot-boat went out to discover the Mosquito: all they could find was the bottom half of a pair of pyjamas wedged under a rock. The next day my parents, sitting down to breakfast and fondly thinking of their son afloat in the Solent, opened their paper to the banner headlines Four Britons Sunk Off Cherbourg.

A gentler 'school trip' was undertaken one spring holiday when four of us accompanied a young classics master to Italy. In those days such trips were revolutionary. The rackety train crawled across drab post-war France and then came the wonder of a midnight halt at a Swiss station; sparklingly clean, brilliantly lit and providing the best café au lait I have ever tasted. This was but a curtain-raiser to discovering Florence, Rome and Pompeii – and the beginning of a love affair with Italy that has held me in thrall ever since.

A fourth event in my senior years related the school to a national event – the death of King George VI. The funeral cortege's journey across London necessitated considerable manpower to line the route. Cadet forces drawn from schools throughout the London area were called upon to fill up the numbers. So it was that a squad of us found ourselves attending an extra early morning parade to learn an unfamiliar drill manoeuvre – 'Standing on Arms Reversed', a drill used only at funerals. This mastered, we set off by coach at dawn a few days later and duly found ourselves a minor part in a major and moving piece of ceremonial. It would have been hard not to be caught up in the profound sense of national grief and loss, not to be seen again until the death of Princess Diana. A year later the mood was reversed with the Queen's coronation: there was a real sense of the dawning of a new Elizabethan era. The Queen's reign has been the backdrop to my adult life – which is no doubt part of the reason why I am an uncritical and sentimental royalist!

My final school year was upon me. I sat for a closed scholarship, with an attached bursary, linking Harrow to Brasenose College, Oxford. I was the only candidate but they still gave me just the bursary. My place was nevertheless secured.

One little obstacle remained – two years of National Service. The word on the street was that the best option was to learn Russian and opt for the Intelligence Corps. This was rumoured to lead to a cushy billet in Paris, perfecting one's Russian with the help of émigré countesses. Fooled by this mythology, I took Russian for a year in the sixth form. The residue of this endeavour was an eight-line poem on freedom by the Russian poet Lermantov, memorised to impress parents at Speech Day. It was to serve me well in the years ahead.

Chapter 4

PLAYING SOLDIERS

T he next stage of my generation's life-journey – or rather steeplechase – was the military water jump. For most of us this represented a total change of life, a whole range of fresh and not always palatable experiences. For many of us it would include being transported to a remote part of the globe to garrison some part of our far-flung but rapidly diminishing empire. For all of us it would mean encountering a fresh ethos, a fresh set of values, though here there were continuities with school life.

Throughout my time at Harrow I had never quite lost my sense of being on the outside and looking in. I had joined the school in fear and trembling, not sure whether I could ever come to belong to it. In time I discovered a part to play and a place to fill and even in time aspired to the eminence of the shiny top hat which singled out the vastly superior School Monitor. Yet I never, deep down, was quite sure that Harrow was me or I was Harrow. I hung loose to much of its ethos.

Indeed, it was difficult in those days to know quite what its ethos was. It had once been the aim to produce 'leaders of empire' but the amount of empire left to be led was diminishing by the year, if not the month. We could still spawn captains of industry, providing involvement in trade was glossed over. Yet there seemed to be a vacuum in the area of overall ideals and motivation for the school.

Like most of our public schools, Harrow was officially Christian, of the Anglican variety. It was required that we attend two out of three chapel services each Sunday and each evening concluded with House Prayers (occasionally followed by the further entertainment of House beatings, as I have recounted). Most boys got confirmed during their time at school and there was an annual recruiting sermon for the ministry ("There are at present two Old Harrovians in Holy Orders in the Diocese of Lincoln. When I die, there will be one.") Somehow it failed to catch fire. And a deficit in Christian values at some points in the school's life was atoned for by zero tolerance in the minutiae of conduct and of manners. There were, of course, conspicuous examples of caring dedication to the job and of Christian faith among the staff but, overall, I felt there had to be something more on offer: subconsciously I was looking for it.

Possibly the most enlightened Act of Parliament of the past 60 years was the Clean Air Act 1956, which cleansed London of its Dickensian fogs. I was at Harrow before all that and each winter the fogs were atrocious. One Sunday evening we went off to evensong mildly titillated by the promise of a visiting preacher. My appointed seat was beneath a tablet to a Crimean War typhoid victim, Eric Duodecimus Fletcher; I knew the wording by heart. That night the view from my seat was different; wisps of mist were already beginning to wreath the altar. The fog was invading the chapel. We watched fascinated. By the time we reached the Magnificat, the choir had disappeared totally. Come the third collect, the pulpit steps were fuzzy. The preacher was already a spectral figure as he ascended them and very soon, to our unmitigated glee, our visitor had totally vanished from view. All that was left was the dull booming sound of the preacher's voice emerging from the fog.

Now I had very little background on the whole Christian thing. My father, bless him, reckoned he had been cured of religion by his experiences in the First World War. We were, therefore, not a church-going family and my sole experience of church had been school religion of relatively low wattage. So it was that our evensong experience that night represented exactly my attitude to the Christian faith: something was going on alright but it came across to me as a dull booming sound coming out of a seemingly impenetrable fog.

So, here I was, without any faith position to undergird me, just leaving a world with regard to which I had at times felt loosely attached and consequently somewhat phoney, and now about to enter another world where, in two years, one could not hope to be more than an amateur in a world of dedicated professionals. Once again it was with considerable misgivings that I set off on foot from home, clutching the Queen's rail warrant and destined for the Royal Artillery's basic training unit at Oswestry in remote north Wales.

Why had I chosen 'The Gunners'? Old school voices would have muttered about selecting either some smart infantry regiment or else a set of socially pre-eminent 'donkey-wallopers', as we rudely called the – now mechanised – cavalry. For me the predominant motive was a teenage obsession with pyrotechnics and a passion for mixing home-made gunpowder. It was time to try the real thing. My ambition to become a Russian-speaking intelligence officer did not survive a preliminary interview at the recruiting office with an elderly ex-Indian Army major. "You don't want to get into any of that damned long-haired stuff. Get out and get your knees brown, boy.. Gullibly, I swallowed this line and my Russian was still-born.

The train journey from East Grinstead to The Gunners' training depot at Oswestry was slow, crowded and depressing. Somebody had translated two years into minutes: it was a lot. It was raining heavily. Our arrival was greeted by keen-faced NCOs waiting to receive us on the platform. We were rapidly 'fell in', marched off, issued with scratchy uniforms and a very large sheet of brown paper. With this we were instructed to wrap our 'civvies' (civilian clothes) for posting home, together with our civilian identities. Allocated to barrack huts, we found ourselves with 40 others packing away kit in dispirited fatigue. Before early 'lights out' an extraordinary thing happened: three or four of our number knelt down by their bunks to say their prayers. I was outraged. How embarrassing! What a public display! What a way to court ridicule! It registered with me that for some people all that sort of thing was obviously important.

Two weeks of being drilled, shouted at, lectured, and taught the intricacies of kit lay-out led us to a parting of the ways – between field and anti-aircraft artillery. I was dispatched with the ack-ack contingent to a desolate camp on the North Welsh coast, at Tonfanau. It was an isolated spot, served only by a single-track railway. Those being demobbed from the camp would pay the engine driver half a crown to make the engine hoot derisively until out of earshot. It was said that out there even the sheep spoke Welsh. The rules of the camp were simple: 'If it moves, salute it. If it doesn't, whitewash it'. This was to be the location for our basic training. But first the potential officers had to be segregated. This was achieved straightforwardly. Our sergeant fell us in and then delivered himself of this order: "All them as reads the Daily Telegraph, one pace step forward march." On this simple rule of thumb our futures were determined and the intelligentsia, thus identified, were formed into 'Z Troop', a *corps d'élite*. The ignoramuses who read only The Times and The Guardian were left behind. I read the Daily Telegraph.

So for 16 weeks we drilled and we polished our kit through basic training. Life in the barrack hut was certainly basic. War is said to be the extension of diplomacy by other means: one might equally have said that the Army was only the extension of school by other means.

I was interested some years later to read a throwaway line by a British industrialist released from captivity at the hands of the Iranian government: "Once you've attended a public school you can put up with pretty well anything."

So far we had – wisely – not been allowed near a gun. From time to time senior initiates fired off the 4.7inch large guns mounted down by the beach, in a vain attempt to hit the drone targets intrepidly towed across the bay by kamikaze pilots desperate for the bounty. We were instead trained on the radar sets built to guide the guns. We spent many a pleasant morning in the motor vans housing the sets, where, out of the eye of authority, we could read our Daily Telegraphs or, through the roof-mounted telescope, gaze admiringly at the camp commandant's daughter as she sunbathed in her garden.

We kept up with our Telegraphs because the next hurdle required it. The War Office Selection Board, or WOSB, was a searching residential test that finally sorted out those destined for officer training. In due course my turn came and I travelled off to my appointed centre, joining another dozen or so hopefuls at a country house near Winchester. The approach was softly, softly and we were treated nearly like adult humans. This was made clear on the first morning, when breakfast offered us coffee and unlimited toast and marmalade – the first we had seen for many months. For the only time in my life naked ambition reared up inside me: I lusted to belong to the toast-eating ranks of the Army. Thus powered, I set to with a will, answering up brightly in interviews, contributing volubly to the group discussion, getting the team to lever an oil drum of 'uranium' over a 'bottomless abyss', and chairing the major incident committee. So assiduously did I put up my smoke-screen that in due course I found myself posted to Mons Officer Cadet Training Unit, Aldershot.

Mons was the whole basic training bit over again, only more so. On our first morning on the parade ground we encountered the doyen of Mons, Regimental Sergeant Major Brittain, Coldstream Guards. A legend in his own lifetime, he had been tethered at Mons like a great hot air balloon (there were points of resemblance) for some years. He surveyed us grimly: "When I gaze at you gentlemen", he roared despairingly, "and then look up at our flag, I pray for our beloved country." He went on to assure us that he would call us 'sir' and we should call him 'sir', but only one of us would be meaning it.

Thus chastened, we faced the next four months grimly. By now I had switched to field artillery, as holding out better offers of overseas postings. The 25-pounder was the standard weapon and we trained on it non-stop until we were finally allowed to tow our guns to Salisbury Plain for a live shoot. The standard charge packed a healthy bang but an extra "Charge 3" bag of propellant cordite could be added to enable you to punch a solid shot through a tank. We were naturally limited to the standard charge. When we came off the gun position, we could see a little circle of gunners squatting on the grass round a kettle. Suddenly a hideous glare briefly lit the group. Two minutes later tea was being served. Spare "Charge 3" bags had their uses.

Eventually we reached the proud day of our commissioning, a day of ice and snow that reduced our final parade to shambles. The commandant sadly remarked that we looked like the retreat from Moscow. We ignored the slur since we were now free to tear the white facings off our uniforms and replace them with a nice, shiny, pip on each shoulder. In due course, the Queen sent a scroll to her 'trusty and well-beloved servants' assuring us of her confidence in our abilities. In my case her confidence was certainly misplaced.

The 'retreat from Moscow'

Where were we to serve? In those palmy days we had all been given a fat brochure of global possibilities to leaf through to select the perfect posting to which that well-established firm of travel agents, HM Queen and Co, would be only too pleased to transport us. Of course, it was not going to work like that but at least we had the illusion of choice. I opted for what was regarded as the plum posting, Hong Kong ("Honkers"). The Queen met me half way and posted me to the 41st Field Regiment in Egypt.

Yet another departure into the unknown, fraught with foreboding, took me from Stansted Airport via Malta to RAF Fayid on the Suez Canal. The warmth and sickly sweet smell of Egypt and the soft chirping of cicadas rose up to meet us as we stepped out of the Dakota. Next morning a drive along a blazing desert road in a truck designed for towing field guns, with an armed sentry peering out of a hole in the roof, brought us to Moascar Garrison and the regiment, located in a tented camp surrounded by coils of barbed wire. Another camp lay the other side of the road and next to us was a military cemetery. Apart from that, flat desert extended in every direction.

At that time, 80,000 troops occupied the Canal Zone, with no very obvious legal justification, to protect our interest in the canal and to free access to our bases further east in East Africa, Malaya and Hong Kong. We were the subject of sporadic 'terrorist' attacks by resentful Egyptians and were technically 'on active service'. So we lived in tented camps out in the desert defended by a wall of concertina wire and frequent guard-posts. Some major defended townships were scattered round to provide married quarters, shops and headquarters.

Into this arid world I was suddenly projected, like an astronaut on to the moon. My dress betrayed me: I was still clad in thick khaki while all around wore khaki drill shorts. An early visit to the Indian tailor rectified this and I gradually became at least sartorially assimilated into the regiment. Life was a blend of training, administration, socialising in the mess and recreation round the shores of Lake Timsah, a natural blip in the Suez Canal that afforded great sailing. The pace was gentle – the climate saw to that. In the hot season work began at 6.00am and ended sharp at noon. Lunch and a 'zizz' (nap) in one's tent would be followed by teatime tennis, sailing or, later on, a film at the open-air cinema. (Colour picture)

The security situation was always a dimension. On my very first morning I was woken by shots from the military cemetery bordering our camp: it was the funeral party firing a salute over the grave of a young British soldier murdered by terrorists, his mutilated corpse thrown on to a rubbish dump: for me, a grim introduction. Every truck and every train had to carry armed sentries and every sentry had to carry his weapon chained to his wrist, to prevent theft. The weapon used was the notorious Sten gun, a light automatic that could discharge a whole magazine at one go, frequently without any help from the owner's trigger finger. Made by the 100,000 for the invasion at a cost of 7 shillings and 6 pence (about 38p) they could be lethal to their users as well as their targets. It was said that our troops sustained more injuries from their own guns in Egypt than ever they did from Egyptian action.

A rare excursion into the desert

Being at the time unconfident and unsure in exercising authority, I was not well suited to regimental life. My troop commander disapproved of me as much as I disliked him. After some months he found a way to dispose of the problem. A vacancy had come about for a junior subaltern to run errands for the brigadier at the headquarters of the 1st Infantry Division. Just the man! I was booted upstairs to headquarters and acquired the grandiose title of Intelligence Officer to the CRA (Commander, Royal Artillery). Although at the time I felt ashamed to be leaving the regiment, in retrospect it was a good move. The new work was more cerebral, offering scope for some individuality. We lived in tents round a rather grand mess actually on the banks of the Great Bitter Lake: and the new Officers Club, with its social life and sailing, was just a quarter of a mile down the road.

And there I served out my time. Memory presents a dish of recollections. There were mess nights under the stars in resplendent mess dress, concluding in a leisured excursion out along the pier that ran from our shoreline into the lake – an exercise that lent a whole new meaning to the phrase 'peer group'.

There was a mission given me by my brigadier, a good man who did not suffer fools gladly, to take his Landrover out to a grid reference in the Sinai Desert, where he would land in our artillery Auster spotter plane to take part in an exercise, leaving me to fly home. The landing-strip was 100 yards of flat gravel and it is not that easy to find a grid reference in a featureless desert. Mercifully, we got it right and a highly relieved subaltern watched his boss descend from the skies before himself enjoying a flight home along the canal.

There were halcyon days spent sailing on the Great Bitter Lake. Ten miles wide, it was actually a sea. In an afternoon a good breeze could waft you from Africa across to Asia. Multi-class races were a thrill, except the boat I used was disconcertingly fast and usually led the pack, but, with me at the helm, often round the wrong buoy.

There were trips to Cairo and Alexandra, once we had signed the agreement with Egypt to withdraw and no security problems remained. There was a most exciting exercise down in the Gulf of Suez. Our evacuation was looming and the ordnance people wanted to get rid of as large a stock of obsolete explosives as possible. The climax of the exercise, therefore, was a simulated atomic explosion that fulfilled even my pyrotechnic ambitions. We were then allowed to bask on deserted beaches that now attract luxury hotels.

And there was our 'Escape and Evasion' exercise in Cyprus, to which three of us were despatched. The scenario was a break-out from a prisoner of war camp on the north coast with a view to trekking to safety 70 miles along the coast. Actually, we were giving the Cyprus forces training for the battle with the Greek Nationalist movement, EOKA, which was clearly looming. Sixty of us, British and American, were deemed to have escaped and were sent off overland. Our little group of three managed 25 hours on the loose before we were rounded up, incarcerated in Kyrenia Castle and fed on bread and water for 48 hours. I have always longed to return under more relaxed conditions, to enjoy a wider view of Kyrenia than is permitted by an arrow slit.

At the conclusion of the exercise we celebrated our release by going out to dinner in Nicosia. We found a magnificent restaurant. It was quite empty: we had it to ourselves and the meal matched the surroundings in splendour. At the end I went up to pay and commented on how empty the place was. "Oh yes, last week someone tossed a hand grenade through the door. It didn't go off but we haven't had many customers since."

Recently survivors of the British troops who served in Egypt during the period of active service have finally been awarded a medal (blocked until now by the Foreign Office for fear of offending Egyptian sensitivities). For most, this was a recognition of service in the Canal Zone. For me, I believe it was acknowledgement of one particular piece of service I was able to render to the Crown. It happened like this.

Until the time the British had signed the agreement to withdraw, we had ridden roughshod over Egyptian Customs requirements and enjoyed cheap drinks in the mess. With the signing we went all legal and paid the tax required: our drinks accordingly doubled in price – clearly an unacceptable situation. In our mess we devised a solution. The divisional artillery had a detached battery in Aqaba in Jordan, a country with which we were on the best of terms. The King was an Old Harrovian, so there was no nonsense about paying Customs duty there. As the sparest subaltern in our headquarters, I was accordingly dispatched to arrange a large-scale smuggling run. Once again I took to the air in our faithful Auster spotter plane and we pottered across the Sinai Desert to Aqaba. The control tower at the landing strip, I recall, was the fuselage of a wrecked Dakota, which did little for one's morale on landing. A well-lubricated luncheon with the officers of the battery sealed the deal. An exchange of telegrams thereafter made much reference to 'battery fluid'. Finally, on the appointed day, I drove down before dawn with a three-ton lorry to an isolated spot on the Gulf of Suez. Anxiously I scanned the horizon. A pinpoint turned into a dot and in time became a landing craft, which beached just below me. Down went the ramp; inside stood six gunners holding their rifles, which for some obscure reason had bayonets fixed: behind them were stacked up row after row of large boxes of 'battery fluid'. Never has a three-ton lorry been so rapidly loaded and driven off. For a week at least my stock stood high in the mess. It was for this achievement, I am sure, that I was awarded my medal.

Perhaps it was the merit I had acquired with my superiors in this way that enabled me to pull off a minor coup when demobilisation drew near. Instead of being tamely sent back in a troop ship to Woolwich, I and a good friend, Pat Wilson (who had followed me from 41st Field to the headquarters), managed to get ourselves posted instead to a regiment in Cyprus and demobbed from there. With a pocketful of demob cash, we set off to make our own way home, to a new life at Oxford. Our horizons had suddenly widened.

Chapter 5

DREAMING SPIRES AND LOST CAUSES

After two years of being cribbed, cabined and confined by Army discipline and horizons, the joy of being let loose on our own, with time and cash enough to trickle our way back across Europe, was almost unimaginable for my travelling companion and myself. This was to be our Grand Tour.

We got off to a bad start when we celebrated our liberation from 'the Queen's Shilling' by dining out at a fish restaurant in Limassol. Next morning we embarked on a Greek ship for Piraeus. By this time I was feeling absolutely awful; the shellfish had been just slightly off. As the voyage progressed I was overtaken by an unbearable sensitivity of the skin that made it impossible so much as to touch the deck with my feet. The ship's medical resources consisted of an ample Italian lady with no English. My tiny pocket dictionary could hardly do justice to the subtleties of my condition (though I retain the Italian for 'bowels' to this day). Unfortunately, my symptoms could have been those of typhoid, so when we docked at Piraeus I had to be cleared by the port's Director of Medical Services before anyone could disembark. He came to inspect me, with most of the passengers pushing into the cabin behind him to have a look. Mercifully, the great man declared that it was food poisoning and took no further interest. The ship emptied like a drain and we limped after our fellow-passengers. A taxi took us to the address of a doctor's surgery we had been given. After one look the doctor filled a syringe large enough for a horse with anti-histamine and plunged it into me. Within a few hours I was cured and the Grand Tour had begun.

We had passed from the deserts and barbed wire of Egypt to the glories of Greece. We duly gazed in awe at the Parthenon and the other splendours of ancient Athens. In 1955 the city was still small, impoverished and pre-industrialised. The tarmac ran out a few streets away from the Royal Palace. Very few hotels served meals, for which you had to go out to a taverna. So naïve were Pat and I that it was three days before we began to puzzle about the frequency of US servicemen passing up and down the stairs of our hotel: they were definitely not looking for board and lodging! By the time we had twigged we were off on a trip by local bus to Delphi. We were getting on fine with our fellow passengers until we swept round a corner to be confronted with the outline of Cyprus carved into the hillside bearing the legend *'Enosis'* (Union) – with Greece! The rest of our journey was conducted in silence.

A boat to Brindisi (breathe in when you go through the Corinth Canal) and a train onwards brought us to Naples. Here we renewed acquaintance with the paralysed drama of Pompeii before we headed on north for a sniff at Rome and a sybaritic wallow in the splendours of Florence. Thence by incredibly uncomfortable train to Dieppe, ferry to Newhaven, and there were my parents waiting with their beloved silver Jaguar. What an auspicious homecoming for someone just about to read Classical Moderations and Litterae Humaniores ('Mods and Greats' for short – Greek and Latin literature, followed by the history of Greece and Rome, with philosophy) at Oxford!

The Army had been a big – and in some ways liberating – experience but it had necessarily been a sideshow. I had indeed succeeded in my ambition to eat toast and marmalade but I was still surprisingly unconfident, anxious about the impression created, lop-sided in a number of ways and unsure what I was meant to be. On my way home I had discovered that Pat was 'one of those Christians', as had been the outstanding NCO in our headquarters. They both seemed to have a solidity and a certainty that I lacked.

Brasenose College that October was a mysterious community to enter, although my brother, Brian, had previously been to Wadham, the first in our family to enter university. When I had come up to the college from school for my entrance exam I had been bemused to see my future tutor, Maurice Platnauer, stumbling across the Old Quad in the morning mist to invigilate us. He was immaculately clad in gown and mortarboard but wearing carpet slippers. He paused on the steps to the dining hall to take a pinch of snuff before entering. There was still more than a whiff of *Zuleika Dobson* about the Oxford of the 50s.

My initial two impressions were, first, the congenial company of my fellows and, second, the immense amount of work we were expected to accomplish. Classical texts that would have occupied us for a term at school had to be completed in a week. Fortunately, Maurice, our tutor, treated us as if we were still schoolboys and inflicted on us a weekly test. The course, as described, had the tedious adjunct of textual criticism tacked on (who cares what was the original manuscript reading?). We were, at the end of it, entered for the longest examination in Europe – 13 three-hour papers, to be faced in our fifth term.

The rigours of academic life

This academic rigour was mitigated by the warmth of friendships that soon sprang up. Most of us had come from National Service, where we had been propping up some disintegrating corner of the British Empire, so we had a fund of experience to pool. One of my best friends I had already met in north Wales; a calm, good-humoured man whose peace of mind came from deep within. His name was Alan Cowling and he turned out to be, unexpectedly, a Christian.

Dinner in Hall, formal though it was (gowns and a long Latin grace), proved a delightful rendezvous with kindred spirits across the disciplines. Clubs and societies competed for our favours; so did sporting teams, but they no longer exerted the moral compulsion that had been so oppressive at school. Here was a community where you were free to be yourself and develop your own thing.

One cloud blighted the dawn of my second year, occasioned by the antics of our government. Anthony Eden wrongly identified Colonel Gamal Abdel Nasser of Egypt as a second Hitler and determined on a Middle Eastern adventure, anticipating George W Bush by 48 years. The blatant dishonesty of the government's case was clear and the execution of the Anglo-French intervention was deplorably delayed. If you are going to do wrong, it is best to do it quickly.

Oxford, with the rest of the country, had time to wake up. Normally politically quiescent at this time to the point of apathy, the University was bitterly divided; Senior Common Room as well as Lower. One day shoals of us, without seeking permission, took off to Westminster to lobby our MPs. At the station the police, entirely *ultra vires*, took our names and sent them in to the don responsible for discipline in each college, for appropriate action. Our Senior Dean, an old-style Liberal, wrote to the Chief Constable to thank him, saying that he would now be able to congratulate each one of us personally.

An interesting comment on the times was provided by one of my co-protesters, who, being half-Egyptian, felt passionately about the issue. Wearing a dirty old mac and a curious pointed trilby, unshaven and with a crazy mad glint in his eye, he looked exactly like Guy Fawkes. The constable on the door of the House of Commons clearly caught the resemblance. Chuckling hugely he said, "What've you got under that mac, sonny, a bomb?" With a further volley of Ho! Ho! Ho!, he opened the door and admitted us.

Back in Brasenose, our normally tolerant society was split down the middle. One night at dinner the Captain of Boats (in charge of the rowing fraternity, ever in the vanguard of reaction) bought everyone a pint of beer and proposed the Loyal Toast. We drank the Queen's health without making any concessions to her ministers' policies.

The Suez operation lurched forward to its miserable conclusion. The Americans showed how little the 'special relationship' was really worth by turning off the petrol tap and we were forced into an ignominious withdrawal. At this point the British stopped pretending we were the world's policemen. The role passed to the USA, which appears to have been rather less successful than we were.

The effect of all this upon me was fundamental. Until this point my security depended upon a sense of the innate decency of British society. God, if He existed, was an Englishman, probably living south of the Watford Gap and most likely voting Conservative. This rosy vision was now shattered. Here were respected politicians lying through their teeth. What was one's life to be based on? My shaky foundations were in ruins.

At the same time an event, unconnected with Suez, gave me another powerful nudge. Leaving the college one night en route for the cinema, I was stopped by a smiling man whom I had identified as one of the 'God Squad'. "Don't go to the cinema," he said. "Come with us and listen to Billy Graham." A rapid calculation told me this change of plan would save me 3 shillings and 6 pence. How wrong I was: it was to be the most expensive decision I would ever take. Nevertheless, I agreed and we headed off to St Aldate's Church.

I had already visited this city centre church. On arrival in Oxford every undergraduate new to the university had received a personalised invitation to lunch on one of three successive days following the first Sunday's sermon. It seemed only fair, therefore, to attend the sermon as well. The church had been packed with undergraduates crowding the windowsills. The message was punchy and related to student life, with liberal doses of humour. I was intrigued.

I was once again fascinated to discover a queue, four deep, winding round the church. We finally got in and in due course Billy spoke. He said nothing new but what he did say was delivered with burning conviction and addressed heart as well as head. The message was, quite simply: 'You can't mess about. The demand Jesus lays on us is unconditional; there are no escape clauses. It's all or nothing.'

That was the message and it was new to me. Previously, I had had faith presented in terms of agreement to a set of statements but not in terms of committing oneself to a relationship with a living person. This was the new and disturbing message that confronted me. Its starkness was modified by some good friends I made who turned out to be committed Christians from opposite ends of the church spectrum – Alan Cowling, already mentioned, a delightful Baptist and son of a Baptist missionary, and Louis van den Berg, of Dutch Roman Catholic origins, with whom I was to share many adventures.

"You can't mess with Jesus," Billy had said, "It's all or nothing." I was scared stiff and determined that for me it would be nothing. I was not going to live my life in some post-Christian twilight. I would strike out and build my own security and value system. And that is how it was for the next year. I resolutely kept away from churches – nasty, dangerous, habit-forming places – and hid myself in a nerd-like existence coping with the vast quantities of Greek and Latin literature being poured over our protesting heads. That year was the most unhappy of my whole life.

The next move came early in the fifth term. I sat down one Sunday evening in Hall, looking forward to a good dispute with an argumentative friend of mine (still my friend!). The conversation turned to religion and my neighbour, a Roman Catholic, set about the Anglican beliefs he thought I held. I made a hollow defence but it revealed to me once again my inner emptiness.

The next morning provoked a crisis. I had an essay to present to my tutor at noon and when I sat down at my desk at 9am my pad was empty. It was still empty at 10am, as all my mental energy was consumed by my inner debate. At 10.30am my nerve cracked: I knelt by my bed and said glumly: "Jesus, if you want me, I'm yours. But please let me get on with this essay." At 11.55am I ran up the High Street, the world's newest disciple, clutching the worst essay ever written in the University of Oxford. As I neared college I noticed the sun shining brilliantly on the gold cross topping St Mary's spire. I had never noticed it before.

Clever theologians are very distrustful of what they call 'sudden conversions' (or, as they term them, 'conversion-experiences', thus booting the matter into a touchline of subjectivity). Pure emotionalism, they say. But such critics are usually agnostics or those who have grown up securely within the Church's sheep-pen and have no sudden turn-round points in their pilgrimage: gradually and over time they might become aware of the Jesus who walks alongside them. They cannot understand what a revolution occurs when someone resolutely headed in one direction is led to execute an about-turn. The two routes into faith might be called respectively the 'road to Emmaus route' and the 'road to Damascus route'. The routes are different but equally valid. The destination is exactly the same.

The results of my modest, deskbound, Damascus Road volte-face were startling and totally unexpected. What had held me back for so long was the fear of a personality take over, a brain-washing that would leave me yet more inhibited and shut in. There were indeed some college Christians, who seemed to me rather dull and grey. But there were other splendid examples who actually seemed to exude *joie-de-vivre*. What had looked to me like death from the outside, turned out to be the beginning of life itself.

In handing myself over to Jesus for disposal, I found myself not enslaved, as I had feared, but actually set free; free to become more myself, not less. The world had suddenly turned from sepia to technicolor, from mono to stereo, from normal to HD.

This is, of course, none other than the classic description of conversion, the human personality being touched by the love of God, the point where faith becomes personal. The benefits that flow from this will to some extent depend on the individual's particular needs. Forgiveness, purpose, integration, confidence, joy, new resources – all these I found and many blessings beside. It is a process I have been privileged to see repeating itself in other lives throughout my ministry.

The immediate results of my discovery were ambivalent. On the one hand I was at once a much happier and more secure person. I was enabled to pass through the dreaded 13 three-hour papers of the Mods exam with relative equanimity and obtained a reputable 2nd class degree. But at the same time the world had become far more fun; now, with my insecurity gone, relating to others became far easier. All this, I was to find, was to the detriment of my studies. St Aldate's turned out to be not just a church building: it was also the focus for a community of lively young men and women that I was happy to join. At that time the religious life at Oxford was in ferment. Droves of us surged off to this church to listen to that bishop, or to so-and-so's room to discuss the Letter to the Romans. A serious generation, which had spent two years of National Service out in the wide world, really wanted to know if there was a purpose to life and whether Christianity could supply the answers. All my opinions, I found, had gone into a sort of kaleidoscope and it was fascinating to discover what I now thought about things. I ventured out into clubs dealing with international affairs and debating: I even, very late one night, delivered a short speech at the Oxford Union.

All this was great but did not really benefit my work. In the sixth term I embarked on the second half of my course. Known as "Greats", it consisted of the history of Greece and Rome combined with philosophy. In other words, where Mods had required you to digest, Greats challenged you to study, analyse and think. I failed to connect with it satisfactorily and found myself more than a little at sea.

If I did not exactly hit the ground running work-wise as I entered the second half of my university course, all the more social aspects of life blossomed and flourished. I rowed, for instance, in a "Gentlemen's Eight" (ie summer only). In those days each college had its own houseboat as base for its oarsmen, moored up alongside the Meadows. It was always said the Brasenose College boat was solidly aground on a bed of beer bottles.

Already in that spring of '56 a large group, 20 of us, had taken off at the end of term to walk off our academic labours by following the Pilgrim's Way from Winchester to Canterbury. The camaraderie was intense, the physical exertion modest. For me it now had particular significance to travel thankfully home to the Mother Church of Anglicanism. The pilgrimage had become real.

We decided to consolidate the *esprit de corps* engendered by this enterprise by making ourselves into a club and giving ourselves a posh title: the Brasenose Peripatetics was born. We took our name from a Greek philosophical school that would 'stroll about' ancient Athens engaged in elevated discussions. It was many years before I learnt from my French sister-in-law that the same title in French was used to describe the Parisian ladies of the night who 'stroll around' for quite other purposes.

That summer the Peripatetics set themselves a more ambitious aim – to meet up in the French Alps and to walk through Andorra into Spain. Before that, however, my friend John Liversedge and I had another commitment – to put in a fortnight helping at a refugee camp in Austria. The going was good then and travelling hundreds of miles by 'autostop' (ie by thumb) was no problem. In those days the hippy trail had not yet been opened up and hitchhiking was not yet a debased activity. So it was that with many adventures but no disasters we whizzed down to Linz. Here a large camp originally set up by Hitler for autobahn constructors now housed the refugee flotsam and jetsam of Europe. The Austrian government was trying to clear the camp and offered a grant to families prepared to go out and build their own home. A couple on their own with a small child would have found this task difficult. Volunteers from an English charity, therefore, were being allotted to each building team to add extra muscle.

It was my delightful fate to be attached to a young family of Volkdeutsch Romanians who had fled west to escape the Russians. Micki and Minnie had spent most of their lives as refugees but seemed quite unwarped by the experience. They had a little girl, *kleine* Minnie, who was a breath of fresh hope for us all. Two beefy workers from the Wills Tobacco Factory at Bristol, a Jewish girl and I gelled with them to form a good team. The only problem was linguistic. They had no English, we had very little German; so we set about creating a 'builders' Esperanto', drawing on German, English and

Latin, which resembled their native Romanian: *"Achtung bricksen, O popule!"* ("Mind out, everyone – bricks!") usually got through.

Housebuilding — not all hard labour

Our fortnight completed, a swift hitchhike brought us to a point in the Alps adjacent to Andorra. Next morning our intrepid group of six set off to climb into the little co-principality, thus outwitting the Andorran security forces, which, we were told, consisted of a brigadier and two constables. A friendly *gendarme* on the French side bade us pay attention *"aux serpents et au brouillard"* ("snakes and fog"). We failed to heed the second injunction and spent two hours executing a great circle back to the lake from which we had started. Despite the false start, by nightfall we were installed in our Andorran pension, all set for a vinous and verbose evening. The next morning a half-day's stroll brought us to the capital village, where we put up at its modest hostelry. At sundown we were sitting at its pavement café on either side of the main – and only – street when the daily bus came in from France. From it stepped a fellow Brasenasal and his brand-new bride. He had vowed to take her on honeymoon to somewhere

where they could be absolutely sure to meet no one they knew. His face was a study as he met the cheers and raised glasses of a large group of fellow Brasenose men. The couple left early next morning.

Two other vacation ventures may be mentioned at this point. In the new world of the church I had entered I came across the Society of Saint Francis, an Anglican order of friars, some of whom were detached to keep in touch with university groups. They appealed to me because they travelled light and radiated benevolence. One of them, Brother Peter, invited me to tea one afternoon, along with one or two others. He began to expound a wonderful opportunity to work with the Franciscans. A small group of them were to lead a mission to a borstal: North Sea Camp, near Boston, Lincolnshire. Wouldn't it be fun if a few undergraduates came along and actually lived alongside the boys, to make contact with them? The idea horrified me but I could see no reputable way of declining.

It was with a heavy heart that some weeks later I bade farewell to my parents (who thought I was mad) and took train to the remote foggy flatlands of Lincolnshire. My fellow undergraduates and I were welcomed by the Franciscans and the governor, who was strongly behind us. Issued with borstal uniform, we were assigned to our dormitories (barrack huts all over again) and left to get on with it. To my surprise, the natives were much more friendly than I had feared. Each morning we were marched out to the nearby coast to gather samphire. Previously, I had encountered this substance only in the pages of *King Lear*, where its collection is described as a 'dreadful trade'. Nothing too dire attended our labours and our evening mission meetings were well-attended ('Progress in Religion' was one of the criteria for early release).

On the last Saturday the governor gave me £1 and entrusted me with a group to take on a cross-country walk. Unfortunately, the group got wind of this beneficence and set their hearts on finding a pub for a pint. A gentle stroll became a tense cross country race to beat closing time. We made it, all of a heap at 5 to 2.00. The regular clientele froze at the sight of our uniforms. It was just like the classic Western film sequence where the bartender slowly reaches under the bar for a shotgun. Quick action was needed. I put on my most refined Oxford accent and asked the landlady if she could possibly serve us the beer, and what would she like for herself? Her face was a study. It cannot be said that the fortnight transformed the borstal but it was certainly an educational high-spot in my four years at Oxford.

In our final long vacation my friend Louis van den Berg and I were seized with the idea of visiting Naples. We had read Morris West's book *Children of the Sun*, about the plight of the street kids in that poverty-stricken city, and the attempts of a priest, Padre Borelli, to help them. This he had done by disguising himself as one of them and then himself living *incognito* on the streets until he had befriended a large group. One day he re-donned his cassock and dog collar, revealed who he was and offered them a home in a ruined church he had been given for the purpose. To meet him sounded interesting but first we needed funds. We had our eyes on a Brasenasal travel grant, which would demand an academically worthy cover story to disguise our romantic intent. We accordingly concocted a high-flown scheme "to study social conditions in Naples". Duly armed with our super-abundant £50 grant we set off.

Naples at that time was a revelation of poverty. Twelve years had done little to heal the scars of war or alleviate the terrible inequalities between rich and poor. The beaches were still covered with a packing-case shantytown, with open sewer-ditches running between the shacks. In the midst of this squalor dwelt a solitary nun. With teeming families, boys were customarily thrust out into the streets to fend for themselves at age 12.

We were accommodated in a bankrupt monastery, which we shared with three Italian priests. Two were saints, the third – the Prior – was a crook who was subsequently arrested for smuggling television sets in through the Vatican. Father Borelli's orphanage nearby was impressive: a community of over 100 boys was cheerfully living in the converted church and learning trade skills. Borelli himself – no beauty with his broken nose – was quiet and definite. Sadly, he constituted too much of a threat to clerical complacency and was driven subsequently to abandon his orders. Our visit was a great experience for us: not even having to eat horsemeat and spaghetti on a very hot evening could mar it.

A subplot of our visit was to form an opinion on the miracle of San Gennaro. The saint had been Bishop of Naples in the 3rd century and, falling victim to a wave of persecution, had been beheaded. A pious old lady in the crowd at his execution had run out with a bowl and collected some of the saint's blood. This was subsequently bottled and kept for the veneration of the faithful. After some lapse of time a remarkable phenomenon was observed. The blood in the bottle, now dry dust, would liquefy on two occasions in the years – the Saint's feast days – when the bottle was held up for public view. On the few occasions when this failed to occur it presaged some disaster about to befall Naples (a safe bet in a city that is chronically disaster-prone).

Our stay coincided with one of the two feast days and we were able to obtain impressive tickets *per assistere al miracolo* (to be present at the miracle). On the appointed day we joined a large crowd pressing into the cathedral. Inside, the atmosphere resembled that of a football match. The front pews were occupied by a vociferous bevy of pensioners know as 'the Aunts of San Gennaro'. Before the service even began they embarked on a low but penetrating chant: "Viva San Gennaro." Eventually, after preliminary hymns and prayers, the Archbishop of Naples took his place behind the altar and lifted up the sacred bottle by the silver brackets that held it top and bottom. He was newly appointed and this was his first 'Gennaro': I thought he looked apprehensive. Slowly he turned the bottle to reveal the dried blood clinging to its side. The tension rose as the dust remained stable and the volume of the chanting rose several decibels. But then, as we watched from the communion rail, a remarkable thing happened. The encrusted dust did indeed begin to liquefy, detaching itself from the bottle's wall and dripping down to the lowest point. At once the cathedral erupted; the Aunts were ecstatic; the organ burst into the loudest *Te Deum* I have ever heard. Naples – and the Archbishop's skin – were safe for another year. I had seen a miracle – but I was not quite sure I believed it. We argued about what we had seen all the way home; travelling in an uncomfortable train back to the Channel, our journey mainly spent lying in the corridor trying to sleep.

Enriched by this amalgam of educational experiences, I turned my face finally towards the pedagogic equivalent of the Last Judgment – our final exams, or 'schools'. Frantic revision into the small hours could not make up for all those times spent pursing good causes or just plain socialising. The first alarm signal came when, walking sombrely away in our academic 'sub-fusc' (dark suit) and discussing the paper we had just faced, I discovered that I had written the answer to one question about the wrong Peloponnesian War. Worse was to come. A *viva voce* examination was offered to me as a lifeline to pull myself up to a higher class: it had the opposite effect. My answer to one question was so incoherent that the kindly examiner asked me to repeat my response "putting in the punctuation". All to no avail. I achieved a

Counting chickens — in sub fusc

resounding 3rd class. I should have left Oxford in deep depression, feeling I was just one more of its lost causes, had it not been for a second marvellous dose of joyful discovery administered to me in the nick of time.

Chapter 6

DECISIONS! DECISIONS! DECISIONS!

During my final year at Brasenose a new and worrying question came to live with me. It was this: what was I going to do with the rest of my life until a merciful old age pension cut in to terminate my dilemma? From the Oxford viewpoint it was difficult to imagine the future as anything other than anti-climactic, a dim half-life trailing off into distant obscurity. Nevertheless, something must be attempted: but what?

Remembering how the Daily Telegraph had facilitated my toast-eating ambitions, I turned to its career ads page. Accountancy? Sales? Local government? Teaching? Nothing lit up. It was true, however, that a faint aura did illuminate opportunities to work overseas. Egypt with the Army had been an eye-opening experience that, by and large, I had enjoyed. There was, in the background, a tiresome nag about being ordained; but I resolutely closed my mind to that. It held no allure whatsoever; quite the reverse. Whoever was going to imprison themselves in that grey world, cast in a role that was either totally inhibiting or, at worst, comic, the stuff of music-hall humour? Certainly it was not going to be me.

Working overseas offered an escape route from what I saw as the deadness of conventional careers at home or the icy grip of church ministry. Accordingly, I entered the selection procedure for the highest tier of the Civil Service, namely the Foreign Service. A rigorous procedure ensued – long written examinations and a spine-chillingly hostile interview panel. I failed resoundingly and came down to earth with a bump;

nevertheless it will always remain an exam I was proud even to have failed. Anyhow, even had I done better, the Foreign Office would not have appointed me, as this depended on obtaining a second-class degree at Oxford. My eventual result placed me in the third class. The Civil Service, as a consolation prize, offered me a post in the administration of a power station in North Wales. This caused a certain amount of ribald mirth among my friends, especially as a recently deposed Russian political leader had just been posted off to Siberian exile to run a power station. I declined the post with dignity.

So it was that I found myself, in my final university year, in a state of mind alternating between panic and depression. One afternoon, exhausted by the labour of revising, I took myself off to the common room and flung myself down in an armchair. Aware that I was sitting on an uncomfortable lump, I reached underneath me and fished out a chunky booklet which proved to be about opportunities available in the British Council (I cannot recommend this as a method of vocational guidance). "That's it," I thought, "a career valiantly promoting Britain abroad in everything but the political sphere." An interview followed with a congenial pipe-smoker in the back room of an Oxford hotel, followed by an encounter with a small group at the Council's London headquarters. This time the atmosphere was decidedly more friendly than at the Foreign Office. I was duly offered a place and accepted gleefully.

By now a further life-changing question hove into view. At the end of my final university term I stayed on for three weeks for a vacation job teaching English to a congenial group of Austrian teenagers. The pay was £30.00. On the last day, driving over Magdalen Bridge in my ancient Ford car, the engine suddenly belched smoke and then died on me. The repair cost precisely £30.00.

However, in this dismal profit and loss account a further event occurred in that three weeks that was to tilt the balance decisively in the direction of profit. Granted an afternoon off from teaching, I went into Oxford city and strolled into a walled garden belonging to Christ Church, where my church, St Aldate's, happened to be holding its summer fête. I rapidly became aware that I was at least 40 years younger than everyone else present, with one exception: an extraordinarily pretty girl, the church secretary, was on duty pouring out the lemonade. Not surprisingly, we got talking. She was called Margaret and, over the coming weeks a lightning romance ensued. This was complicated by the fact that, after I began work at the British Council, every weekend became a three-way steeplechase. Our family roots were so strong that we felt obliged to see both families each weekend. This meant my meeting Margaret off the train at Paddington before whizzing off either to her parents at West Wickham or mine at East Grinstead. On Sunday we would descend for tea on the other set of parents, before embarking on the drive to Oxford. I would then return to my Chelsea digs by midnight, exhausted.

The British Council, having first intended to post me to Uganda in November, now changed its mind and decided instead to send me to Sudan in January. As preparation I was to be enrolled in a basic course in Arabic at the School of Oriental and African Studies. This consorted ill with the hectic pattern of our courtship. I was not at my brightest when confronted with Arabic irregular verbs first thing on a Monday morning.

Partly because the pace was so punishing and partly because of the extension of time provided by my change of posting, I resolved to bring matters to a head. We had been invited to the engagement party of the sister of my old Oxford friend John Liversedge. This was held at the family's country home near

Sevenoaks. Leading Margaret out into the garden on that unusually warm September evening, I found a grassy bank where we could sit down (only later did we discover that it was in fact, a compost heap). Here I proposed marriage and was, to my delight, accepted. We returned rapturously to the party, blissfully blind to our insensitivity in thus trumping our friends' own celebration.

Leaving the party later, we drove down to Eastbourne's Beachy Head to see in the dawn. My father had unwisely lent me his magnificent Jaguar to drive for the evening: on the way back to East Grinstead I coaxed 100 miles per hour out of it on the dual carriageway. This memorable night ended with our attending the 8.00am service at East Grinstead parish church, Margaret in her party dress and me in dinner jacket and bedraggled bow tie.

We now had to move fast if we were to get married, obtain British Council co-operation to enable us to go out to Khartoum as a married couple and make all necessary preparations to those ends. Fortunately, both families were behind us and were highly supportive. Fast footwork organised the wedding service at Margaret's parents' much loved church at Hayes, Kent. The service itself was taken by the vicar, while Margaret's boss, the Rector of St Aldate's, Canon Keith de Berry, preached.

High winds and lashing rain were quite unable to mar the event. Afterward, our Morris whizzed us off to a Dover hotel, ready for the next morning's ferry to France and the train to Paris. So windy was it that the windscreen wipers blew inside out as we waited on the quayside.

On return, we had time to enjoy a family Christmas before heading off to Liverpool and the SS Salween, which was to take us to Port Sudan. Our departure was overcast by the cancer operation my mother had undergone some months previously.

We hoped for the best. Never-theless, it was with some sadness and anxiety for the future that we headed north up the miraculous M1 – the UK's first motorway and only just opened. Abandoning our brand new Morris Minor to the shippers, we boarded what was to be our floating home for the next fortnight. We were

Our wedding day — the right decision!

greeted by a wonderful discovery: our cabin had been transformed by our parents into a hothouse of flowers and fruits, a delightful leaving present to send us on our way. (Colour picture)

Even at that time it was something of an anachronism to travel out to our overseas posting by ship. The Salween was a small, elderly vessel, part cargo, part passengers. The crew were mainly Indian, the officers British. After a highly unpleasant passage through the Bay of Biscay we entered the tranquil warmth of the Mediterranean. Each day we paced the deck to keep fit, earnestly chanting fragments of Arabic. At noon we made the acquaintance of what was to become a lifelong friend – lager and lime. We solemnly took part in the daily sweepstake on the ship's progress and assiduously played deck quoits. Of our fellow passengers we got to know a few: a nice doctor going out to work in the Emirates; an endearing little Burmese girl with a polysyllabic name that reduced to "Rose"; and an elderly American toper who had signed on for the trip so that he could booze 24/7.

Eventually we passed through the well-remembered Suez Canal, after a disturbing spell ashore at Port Said, where a dubious local 'magician' or 'gully-gully man' offered to make Margaret 'disappear' for just a few piastres. We enjoyed the period charm of the Simon Artz department store, redolent of the 1920s. There was not much on the shelves to buy, though I recall a stack of dusty solar topees. Overhead your change was whizzed from the cashier to the counter in a pot, by means of a complicated arrangement of wires and springs.

When it was time to return to the ship, we hired a man with a small boat to row us back. Halfway across the water he laid down his oars and stated: "You pay me more or I no take you to ship." I glared at him and replied, "You take me to ship or I throw you in canal," After a silent battle of wills he picked up the oars and, to my relief, sullenly resumed work.

On our eventual arrival, Port Sudan turned out be a good harbour backed by low-roofed buildings leading out into scruffy desert. It had been built a few decades back to replace the old Turkish port of Suakin, now silted up. We were rowed ashore, looking back nostalgically at the solid security of the Salween.

Our major decisions were about to be tested.

Chapter 7

GOD'S LAUGHTER

Once on shore we met the British Council in the shape of my new boss, a fussy little man with a deficiency in the humour department. We went to sleep in the government guest house to the chirping of cicadas and woke up to a riot: a Roman Catholic priest teaching at the Catholic secondary school had been framed: seeing a boy ostentatiously reading a book in class, he had thrown the offending volume on the floor. The book, of course, was found to be a copy of the Koran. It was an illuminating introduction to inter-faith relationships.

Before leaving Port Sudan I went with my boss to pay a courtesy call on the mayor. He proved to be a sophisticated gentleman who introduced himself genially with the words: "I am one of Kipling's fuzzy-wuzzies." These were the wild men of the Red Sea Hills who had fought against Field Marshal Herbert Kitchener's invading troops in 1896. Their descendants, still wild, mostly worked as dock-labourers.

The flight to Khartoum in an elderly Dakota proved to be bumpy, nauseating and painful on the ear-drums. As we came in to land we could see the vivid dark green strip of cultivation along the banks of the Nile, sharply distinct from the bleak, rocky desert stretching away into the distance. We were met by the wife of my boss – a tall, stout lady who towered over her husband. She too was fussy and humourless. Together they took us out to quite a pleasant little bungalow in the suburb on the edge of the desert, and there they left us, cast up, high and dry. Baffled and battered, we took stock. On the plus side, we had a

56

neat bungalow, well whitewashed and apparently solid (it was only later that we discovered that actually it was a whited sepulchre built of mud, straw and donkey dung and liable to melt in the rainy season). (Colour picture) It stood in a small garden surrounded by a high wall. With the bungalow came our cook and general factotum, Ali, willing to help but in some areas, notably electrical safety, quite clueless. They were difficult first days, especially for Margaret, who was left virtually a prisoner until, in time, our car and luggage arrived. I meanwhile was whisked away every morning by my boss, who arrived in a large chauffeur-driven car. The driver was instructed to hoot imperiously if he was held up as much as a second.

The British Council at that time worked on a minimal budget and was spread thin around the world. Its remit was to represent Britain in everything but the political sector. Much derided by the press, for the most part it did a good job. At its more solid end it fostered the teaching of English and provided access to English examinations. We imported lecturers on all manner of topics and exported Sudanese scholars to study in the UK. It was perhaps in the strictly cultural area of our activities that we became somewhat detached, even at times a little surreal.

If the Council's work was diverse, ranging from solid technical aid to the artistic airy-fairy, so too were its personnel. Former colonial civil servants, bounced from their desks by burgeoning independence movements, jostled effete young men with a penchant for the ballet. In the Sudan our work consisted of running an office in cosmopolitan Khartoum and operating a library out in the city of Omdurman. This was a great facility in a country where even libraries in Arabic were in short supply. It was much used by a whole range of students working to take UK exams. In those days Sudanese secondary schools took Cambridge GCE exams, so we took care to support their English syllabus. This we did either by showing the appropriate film of that year's GCE set play (Henry V went down a treat, reminding them of their own recent history) or by staging a play-reading.

Into this world I was now introduced and gradually assimilated. At an early stage I went across to the Omdurman Library one evening. To get some idea of the clientele I took over the librarian's seat and set about discovering who borrowed what. No sooner was I on my own than a terrifying apparition materialised and stood before my desk. He was a tall Sudanese from one of the Nilotic tribes, standing nearly 7ft tall, with three rows of tribal markings picked out on his forehead. He was clad in a dirty white shirt and torn shorts. I felt sure he had left his spear on the verandah while he came in to recce the whereabouts of the cash box. Instead, towering above me, he enquired mildly: "Do you have anything else by Neville Shute? I did so enjoy his last book." From the Stone Age to Neville Shute in one colossal bound! Such anomalies were common: as somebody put it, "God laughed when He made the Sudan".

My routine office work was broken up by occasional forays out into the provinces. We aimed to have a British teacher of English in every secondary school stream and part of my remit was to keep in touch with them. In some cases you could well understand why they were teaching in Sudan rather than Sidcup. One of the most exotic was married to an Ethiopian prostitute and spent most of his time illegally brewing beer at home.

While visiting the (fairly few) secondary schools, I would whenever possible take with me in the Landrover one of our films, so I could introduce a show. I remember an idyllic evening down at Port Sudan setting up one such show. We used the football pitch with a sheet draped over the goal post for screen and the Landrover's dynamo providing the electricity. That evening the film was *Genevieve* and the boys were enthralled by that gently humorous saga of the London to Brighton vintage car race. I congratulated myself on a highly successful evening – at least until I met the headmaster the next morning. "Would you please call on the Islamic master?" he said grimly. "He is most displeased."

The Islamic master, I knew, was Egyptian and therefore, by definition, anti-British. I entered his study with some trepidation. "What was the matter with the film?" I asked him. "It was pornographic," he declared firmly. I was dumbfounded. "*Genevieve*? Pornographic? How was it pornographic?" I asked. The answer was both tense and sharp: "It showed a man kissing his wife."

Sometimes I was dispatched by plane to provincial towns where we hoped to establish libraries – Wad Medani, Atbara, El Obeid. Returning to Khartoum, usually airsick after a hot and bumpy flight, I would find Margaret with our little dog Judy waiting to welcome me on the airport balcony. To celebrate these joyful homecomings we always had éclairs for tea in the airport restaurant as a special treat.

One particular chain of events impacted on our normal pattern of work: the major powers got themselves into a sort of cultural arms race designed to impress the Sudanese. The Chinese sent a team of jugglers; the Indians retaliated with a troupe of dancers (the audience left after the first five hours); the Russians despatched some perspiring Cossacks in baggy trousers to perform in the heat. But it was left to the Americans to steal the show: they sent skaters for a show on ice in the midst of 100 degree plus summer weather. Immense technological expertise was deployed to keep the arena frozen for the evening and they largely succeeded. The Sudanese, who had never seen more ice than the lump in a cold drink, turned up in their hordes to see the marvel. Heavily veiled ladies and men by the thousand came to feast their eyes on the scantily clad girls cavorting around on the ice. It was a great success.

How were we to follow that? Our Representative summoned an emergency meeting of the four UK staff to plan our riposte. He explained that he deplored the vulgarity of the mass appeal of the American effort; our own approach was to the intelligentsia, not the mass. He had therefore asked London to send us out a display illustrating the sculptures of Henry Moore. A stunned silence followed this announcement. When the great opening day eventually arrived, the exhibition was sensibly preceded by a drinks party with plenty of whisky flowing to deaden the critical faculty. Only then were the small group of dazed headmasters and civil servants permitted to gaze stupefied at our meagre collection of ladies with holes in their tummies and men with two heads. Both alcohol and the representation of the human form are, of course, anathema to Muslims.

Life was harder for Margaret, without a ready-made role. She, however, did well in finding her own way. She found a post as secretary to the managing director of a British company and performed sterling service in a voluntary capacity by doing typing work for the Anglican Bishop, Oliver Allison, during his visits to Khartoum, and similarly assisted the Reverend John Brown at Church Mission Society headquarters in Khartoum. Her final post was to assist at the British primary school.

Out of office hours we did our best to get into expatriate social life, though we made a few rewarding Sudanese friendships as well. British life revolved around the Sudan Club (Rule 1: All members must be British; no Sudanese guests are permitted). Its president, Margaret's boss, was a leading businessman and straight as a die, revered by his Sudanese staff, a pillar of the Anglican Cathedral, and quite humourless. In a club debate about putting the premises on to the new main drainage system, he caused much unintended mirth by pronouncing: "Our only concern is to put the matter through the proper channels." Apart from its drainage arrangements the club offered a swimming pool, cool, shady lawns and tall Sudanese servants in turbans and white robes called jallabiyahs, flitting noiselessly between lawn and bar. It was a one-race, one-colour (except for servants) oasis. (The scandal when the wife of a new arrival called Smith turned out to be West Indian can well be imagined!). The annual Christmas pantomime packed out the club. Margaret had a major part in it – she was the prompter.

Apart from the club, we sailed and raced on the Nile (the "club house" was one of Kitchener's former gun-boats) (Colour picture) and shared the life of the cathedral, where we sang in the choir. Here, the main aim appeared to be not under any circumstances to permit the lesson-reading to slip from the clutches of the British Embassy into the open hands of the Americans. We usually won. And oh, the joy, when, two Sundays running, a bat flew into an fan above the heads of the American contingent.

Life had now settled down into a regular pattern of my desk work at the British Council enlivened by occasional Landrover journeys out to the secondary schools or flights to check progress at our three provincial libraries. On the home front we entertained (always hazardous with Ali in the kitchen), met friends at the Sudan Club, or took part in the somewhat torpid life of the cathedral. We sailed, and sometimes left the tarmac at the edge of town to drive out into the stony desert for a picnic. Once we went north from Omdurman to the site of the 1898 battle of that name, only to realise that our visit was on the actual date of the bloody encounter. We imagined Kitchener glaring at us from the river bank in fury, impatient to open fire.

A spell of local leave broke this pattern and we determined to spend it in the cool, up in the mountains of Eritrea. The Sunday before departing we entertained an old Sudan hand to lunch. He pooh-poohed the idea of flying and suggested we drove instead. Gullibly, we accepted this notion and duly set out in our little Morris 1000, accompanied by Judy the dog, to drive the 300 miles across the desert to Kassala and on to the Eritrean frontier.

The first night was a disaster. For fear of scorpions, we determined to sleep in the car. Our dog was to stand guard outside, tied to a jerrican. She, however, had different ideas. More nervous than we were, she bounded across the sand to the car, dragging the can behind her. In the end there was nothing for it but to let her in too. It was terribly hot and we shed everything that decency permitted, and quite a lot more as well. Still hot, we opened the car door but found this automatically turned on the light. We had a choice, either to shut the doors and boil or open them and become a peep show for any passing Arab – and in the pitch blackness there were nevertheless a number of people about. We passed an uneasy night.

Next day we got into our drive proper. The Khartoum skyline receded and it became very lonely. The 'road' was a gravel track a quarter of a mile wide, where the truck convoys had found the best path. We had a map but it was of limited use. It was virtually blank, rather like the map in Lewis Carroll's *The Hunting of the Snark*, its only detail afforded by a small dot in the bottom left hand corner with the legend 'Captain Armstrong found water here in 1912'. The surface of the desert was hard gravel, which was fine except that every so often it would become corrugated for long distances. Here all you could do to achieve a smooth ride was to accelerate to 30 miles per hour. which was all right until you encountered a deep ditch.

However, by midnight we reached our destination, the provincial capital, Kassala.

Here we met an unexpected hazard: the town was totally surrounded by a row of 4ft high concrete posts, too close to one another to permit a car to pass. We drove slowly round the perimeter but somehow missed the road entrance. Eventually, exhausted, I found a loose post and plucked it out of the ground. We drove into Kassala in triumph and even found the government rest house, where we were able to doss down. We awoke to find the sun high and a chorus of pigeons serenading us from tall trees around.

Much encouraged by our success, we drove on to the frontier between Sudan and what was then Ethiopia. Now we were on real tarmac roads leading up into cool, green mountains. In the late afternoon we passed Keren and set out on the final stretch to the city of Asmara. We had been warned to be off the road by early evening to avoid the local villains, appropriately called *shiftas*, and I was getting anxious. Rounding a corner, we saw to our relief a substantial police post. It was only when we reached it that I saw it was empty and pock-marked with bullet holes. However, not long afterwards we reached the safety of Asmara, then the provincial capital, a bright sophisticated town owing much to the years of Italian occupation. Here we put up at a little guest-house for Italian commercial travellers; only my Italian pocket dictionary saved us from ordering goat for supper.

Our subsequent week in the green and the cool was absolute bliss and set us up for the weeks ahead. For our return drive across the desert, (now encumbered by a Christmas tree Margaret had lifted from a roadside wood before we left) we determined to travel by night to take advantage of the cool. Halfway across the desert track to Khartoum there was a low hill and here some entrepreneur had established a coffee shop.

We joined the motley group of truck-drivers, who made us most welcome. After our coffee they came out to see us off and collapsed into helpless mirth, slapping their thighs with delight when they saw our little Morris.

Back in Khartoum, our home-made social life continued with unabated vigour. A notable event was the celebration of Margaret's 21st birthday with a group of friends out in the desert, where we contrived to dance an eightsome reel. Suddenly, from nowhere we were joined by a group of Sudanese with their basic lute-like instruments (made from a gourd and fusewire strings).

Another night we were invited to a party embodying a treasure-hunt round central Khartoum. We duly set off in a number of car-loads to follow the clues, Margaret in one car, I in another. One clue was to note the date on the telegraph pole next to the gate of the Egyptian Embassy. Little had the organisers reckoned on the visit of the Egyptian president the next day. The sentry was therefore on high alert – that is to say, he was awake. The arrival of a car-load of torch-flashing Brits worried him greatly, so that when the second car turned up he acted: he rang in to the embassy to report these sinister happenings. The Third Secretary, arriving in his dressing gown in time to witness a further invasion, at once rang the police. I turned up in the car behind Margaret's, just in time to see her being hoisted into the back of a 3 ton lorry full of tall riot police with tin hats and long staves. "Drive on," she shouted to us – so we did. As soon as possible I got hold of my own car and followed Margaret to the police station. Fortunately, there was an inspector on duty who had attended a course at Hendon and understood the strange ways of the Brits. Nevertheless, it was nearly midnight before I obtained her release and we could return to the party. Nobody had kept us any supper. The next morning I reported to my boss that my wife had been arrested for espionage. He was not amused. "I shouldn't have anything to do with that sort of thing if I were you," he said. I never discovered whether he meant marriage or espionage.

By now we had nearly completed our two year tour of duty and home leave beckoned. Margaret was expecting our first child – an added inducement to head for home. The British Council's activities – or at least their weirder manifestations – had lost much of their allure for me but, far worse, that awful nagging thought about ordination had refused to go away; in fact, it had grown stronger. I was already, in my work, a sort of missionary for the British way of life: ought I to find out if I was meant to be a missionary for the Christian faith? With a heavy heart I resigned from the Council, with its generous salary and attractive perks; on my next posting I would even have reached the grade that entitled me to a hat-rack and a hair-cord carpet.

I had told my boss of my intention, rather rashly choosing a moment when we were bumping across a shimmering desert in a fly-infested taxi. Nevertheless, he was the cathedral organist and presumably therefore sympathetic to the cause. When I told him I was leaving and why, his response was a cross: "Whatever for?" I also saw the cathedral provost, who was almost as discouraging. The only person in favour was Margaret.

With a sense of doom I wrote off to the Church's Advisory Council for the Ministry and requested a selection conference. The die was cast. Another major decision had been taken.

Chapter 8

BACK TO SCHOOL

Our return to the UK now filled our thoughts. Margaret had to travel first because of her pregnancy, so we arranged a passage by sea from Port Sudan. When the time came we enjoyed a lengthy and leisurely journey by rail over the Red Sea hills and down the coast. The train's speed was limited to a very gentle pace as the track was laid on sand. Each coach carried its own cook, who would make tea on request on a little charcoal burner at the rear of the coach. Eventually we got to Port Sudan and I saw Margaret duly installed in her cabin. My own journey back to Khartoum seemed even longer.

There ensued a weary couple of months of separation until the day when I was due to return home too, in my case by aircraft. I was booked on a Comet, the revolutionary aeroplane that would have given Britain a head start in air travel had a design fault not brought one down in the sea off Sicily. All that was still in the future and it was with considerable excitement that I walked across the tarmac to the gleaming plane. The steward met me on the steps with the words "I'm terribly sorry, Sir." My heart sank but he continued "We're overbooked on second class: would you mind travelling first?" I graciously consented and enjoyed a marvellously swift and smooth flight. Landing at Heathrow in the midday sunshine was a dream. I had forgotten the world could be so green. I was met by my parents and a rather large Margaret and we drove away in the much-prized Jag, still running well despite its ill-treatment on our engagement night.

Whatever the result of my church selection conference might prove to be, I should have to find a job for a year before I could enter a theological college, if that was to be the future. For now the obvious choice was teaching, which in those days demanded no special training in the case of a graduate. On the evening of our arrival at our East Grinstead home I purchased a little second hand car and the next morning Margaret and I set off on a tour of teaching post opportunities. By now we were into the summer holidays, so any headmaster with a vacancy still to fill was becoming desperate. At one school I was offered the post of Head of Department in English: "We can't give you the salary, of course, but you can have the work". Eventually we landed up in a sleepy grammar school in Newquay, Cornwall, complete with a cottage by the beach in the adjacent – and then still delightful – village of Crantock. The rent was £4 per week. We took it.

Now for the Church and the chance to get the ordination notion out of my hair for good. I duly attended a residential selection conference in a retreat house near St Albans. It was much like the Army selection conference but without the toast-eating incentive. The tests were different: instead of leading a team manhandling a barrel of high explosive over a ravine, one was required to chair a meeting engaged in setting up a youth club. Instead of an evening socialising at a bar, there was compline. I had gone to the conference devoutly hoping I would not be recommended for the ministry and so would be set free to get on with life: to my dismay, I was selected for training to become a clergyman. My fate was sealed.

Meanwhile, family matters supervened. In August, in an inefficient and old-fashioned maternity home, Margaret produced a beautiful little girl – the first of our amazing family, who have brought us so much joy. Much anxious study of a

67

book of names had already yielded up Helen Elizabeth Rosalind. Within two weeks Helen was baptised by Margaret's brother, John, and the three of us had set off, crammed into our small car, to drive to Newquay and, as recorded, a new life by the sea.

The transition from visiting Sudanese secondary schools as an honoured guest to teaching English to the second form provided a sharp and salutary contrast. I had exchanged diplomatic cocktail parties for coffee in the staff room. I had also halved my salary in the process.

Newquay Grammar School was an unhappy marriage of two schools a quarter of a mile apart and separated by a bus station. This distance provided an ideal opportunity for dawdling between classes – an opportunity seized by staff as well as pupils. The atmosphere was generally sleepy. I rapidly learnt that the school had three streams of entrants. First were the children of boarding-house keepers, mainly from the Midlands; solid and hardworking but missing for most of the summer term, when the holiday season demanded their presence at home. Then there was a mercurial tier drawn from the families of RAF St Mawgan, probably joining us after half a dozen schools overseas. They tended to produce both the brightest and also the most wicked element of the school. They too left us in the summer, to take up lucrative posts as beach photographers or ice-cream sellers. Lastly, there were the indigenous Cornish, from the farms; not the brightest, and once again withdrawn from school during the summer, for harvest duties. The school could be a lonely place during August.

I was given Class 2B, some 30 13- to 14-year-olds. I enjoyed them: they were polite, bright and keen. It was not until the third year that voluntary apartheid set in between the boys and the girls, who now sat apart. It was at this stage that it became uncool to be keen. English, Latin and Religious Education were the subjects I taught, without myself having any professional training whatever. I coped most of the time but never seized the disciplinary upper hand with 4D, with whom I suffered a double period last thing on a Friday afternoon. Occasionally I was allowed to do quality stuff with the 6th form, although I rarely regained lost ground with them from the time when, having delivered a stern rebuke for their idleness, I spoilt the effect by making a dignified exit into the broom cupboard. I at any rate learnt quite a lot from my year at Newquay Grammar School.

Meanwhile our home situation was in some ways good. The cottage was delightful, with a flat roof over the garage from where you could look out across the sand dunes to the sea. A five minute stroll led to the vast expanse of Crantock beach, saved from the sprawling suburbs of Newquay by the Gannel Estuary. The village had charm – a rare Cornish commodity – an old pub, The Albion; and a grey stone church with a rood screen. Again, however, Margaret was as much a prisoner as she had been in Khartoum. She did her best. Each week she took Helen to the butcher, to be weighed on a sheet of greaseproof and to be quoted a price per pound. She joined the Women's Institute and won the best-dressed clothes-peg competition.

At weekends we explored Cornwall. On Sunday we sang in the choir and in time Margaret taught the Sunday school in a small hut in the churchyard. On one occasion she looked up and found she had more mice in the class than children! We compensated for loneliness by inviting family and friends down. It was particularly good to see my mother, though she was locked into what proved to be a losing battle with cancer. I had had qualms about taking a job so far from East Grinstead but it was the right post.

The year in Cornwall was a year in limbo. Over it hung the theological training ahead and for this it was necessary to obtain a place at a college. My roots at St Aldate's were evangelical but our Crantock vicar, Father Brown, was distinctly Anglo-Catholic. Even when gardening he wore his dog-collar and, of course, his wellies were black. He urged us to try Wells and Queens, Birmingham. The experience was discouraging. So we waited until we had the opportunity to visit Ridley Hall, Cambridge. This felt much better, so we duly signed up; matrimony and even parenthood were recognised states of life there. This was important at a time when the two archbishops of Canterbury and York had just issued a King Canute letter of surpassing silliness, cautioning ordinands not to marry until after college. It was a blend of bad medieval theology and 20th century poverty. Very properly, most ordinands paid no attention to it at all.

After a summer of suspended animation we set off once more, this time to the fen country. Here we settled into digs with the daughter of an eminent atomic physicist. We occupied the basement of a large and gloomy house. Physically, she had the top two floors; psychologically she inhabited a more gracious age (the broom cupboard was always "the butler's pantry"). Ridley was congenial and the teaching good – Old and New Testaments; doctrine; Church history; liturgy, with some practical subjects such as ounselling and preaching tacked on to a crowded syllabus.

The changeover from marking essays to writing them was no doubt salutary. The method for helping us to preach effectively was probably the most effective; it was called "Bouquets and Brickbats". Small syndicates of no more than half a dozen would cycle out through Cambridgeshire's flat fields of rotting cabbages to some remote parish where heresy could do no possible harm. Here one of the group would deliver his first sermon. The next morning the group would reassemble in their tutor's room; after a few perfunctory compliments, they would turn with relish to the task of tearing the unfortunate preacher's words to shreds. Despite this time of reckoning, we enjoyed these outings, even though sad situations were sometimes uncovered. In one tiny hamlet a scratching at the door heralded the irruption of the vicar's door during the second hymn, making a 25 per cent increase in the size of the congregation of four. Another destination sounded more like instructions on how to preach rather than the name of an ecclesiastical area: the benefice was called Gravely with Yelling.

Ridley Hall was presided over by the benign figure of Cyril Bowles, a man of kindliness mixed with cunning. Apparently a confirmed bachelor, he did let slip that this was only because Miss Right had yet to appear. Shortly after this pronouncement, he introduced a visiting lecturer on the social services with the words "We welcome Miss Wright...". The rest was drowned with our laughter, to the bafflement of our visitor. However, in due course, he did marry – a hospital matron, while he himself was consecrated bishop. They made a formidable couple.

So it was that we struggled towards our goal – GOE, the General Ordination Examination, commonly known to us as "God's Own Exam". Gradually, I discovered an enthusiasm for our course and the future did not look quite so black. I recognised an urge within me to communicate the Christian message. Nevertheless, big areas of uncertainty remained. This was made worse by the fact that my parents were completely baffled by my change of direction – doubly hard because getting me through Harrow and Oxford had meant real financial sacrifice for them. Nevertheless, my father stumped up once again with a covenant of £18 per month – a lifeline by the values of the time.

My mother's condition now deteriorated rapidly, though she did have the pleasure of being able to attend Helen's first birthday party. Eventually we left Ridley to move back into my family's Sussex home to help out for her last weeks. The end, when it came, was peaceful. Her cremation service was beautifully taken by Margaret's brother, John. Sadly, we left my desolated father to rattle around in the empty house.

A welcome lift to the spirits was afforded by the arrival of our second daughter, precious dark-eyed Kate. We gave her three names too – Katharine Mary Frances (names are free!). Money was extremely tight and it was a bad day when we had to sell our car. To visit Margaret in the maternity hospital I had to borrow a fellow student's car and tank it up with half a gallon of petrol (I can still remember the expression on the pump attendant's face).

Although the midwife mistook me, gowned in white, for the doctor and would ask me searching medical questions, Kate arrived safely and was much enjoyed by the three of us and our dog, Pandy, who had joined us in Cornwall and appointed herself nursemaid to the girls. To alleviate our poverty, Margaret took in typing from a wealthy Chinese student, while I led tours of Cambridge (how low can an Oxford man sink?). Despite our bizarre, restricted lifestyle we enjoyed Cambridge. The Backs in summer were a delight and in winter candlelit carols from King's College Chapel were a pure enchantment.

Our two years were passing and we had to find a parish for my first curacy; in the Church of England you cannot be ordained without a parish to go to. After earnest consultations with Cyril and visits to a number of possible churches, we finally plumped for Chesham in Buckinghamshire, a sleepy hollow jerked into the 20th century by the extension of the Metropolitan Underground line. It was in the over large Diocese of Oxford and so my ordination was to be in Christ Church Cathedral, aka the chapel of that great college. Right to the end of my time at Ridley I remained uncertain about whether I was doing the right thing. When the ecclesiastical tailor visited the college to measure us for our dog-collars, I saw a strong parallel to the visit paid by the hangman the night before execution to measure your neck for the rope. So it remained until the pre-ordination retreat. I had now acquired a small scooter, complete with a golden "skid lid". As I puttered away from the college the sun came out and all doubts were dispelled about the rightness of this momentous step. Since that time I have been much too busy to give the matter much consideration.

The ordination itself was a great and grand occasion, with a large congregation, made up of the doting families of candidates, packed into the awkward confines of the cathedral. Up in the choir stalls, I looked across at a figure in the stall opposite, shrouded in a jacket and looking a bit like a gargoyle: it was Alastair Whitelaw, our New Zealand friend, whom I had imagined to be tucked up safely in the southern hemisphere. I was touched that he had made such a great effort to be with us.

After the service the former ordinands emerged into the sunshine of Tom Quad as brand new deacons. (Colour picture) The diaconate of the Church of England is a further probationary year, until a second service of priesting. Once again I was wearing the L-plates I had so recently discarded from my scooter. In many ways it seemed as if I had been wearing L-plates all my life.

Chapter 9

GOOD IN PARTS:
THE CURATE'S LOT

L ife within the Church of England's ministry is extremely diverse. We have a better right than that scurrilous former tabloid The News of the World to its sales slogan 'All human life is there'. We touch people at the peaks and troughs of life – marriage and the arrival of new life, delight and happiness, as well as sickness and sadness. On the one hand, I have stood with parents in a hospital side ward when they gave the instruction to switch off the life-support system keeping alive their brain-damaged teenage daughter: on the other, I have had a rocket launched from the church roof in a *feu-de-joie* over the heads of a crowd wildly celebrating the new millennium. Above all, there has been the privilege of continuous pastoral contact with hundreds of individuals and families.

If the ministry is diverse, so is its location. In that mixture of freedom and choice, responsibility and authority that is the Church of England's true ethos, clergy are able to choose to serve wherever seems right. So it is appropriate to launch into a survey of the opening chapters of a man's career by looking at the places where it was worked out.

As related, we started off in Chesham, a curious, tucked-away traffic jam in a valley in the Chilterns, northwest of London. Historically, the area was remote from authority, a good place for people who wanted to keep their heads down or to live outside the law (hence the retirement post for MPs to become 'Warden of the Chiltern Hundreds' because it was an

74

area demanding a special official to police it). This ancient history lived on in the 1960s in the prevalence of Quakers and Baptists, once people who would have suffered a degree of persecution elsewhere. Chesham, in fact, was noted for 'boots, brushes and Baptists'. Four Baptist chapels, divided by family dynasties and feuds rather than by doctrine, glared at each other across the High Street. The native population had been swollen by waves of immigrants when the London Underground struggled out to reach the town. First came the Pakistanis and then, harder to assimilate, overspill people from Wembley. There was a beautiful old parish church in the centre, with four satellite worship centres out in the suburbs and villages. Church life was encouraging and the vicar, Eric Arnold, was an effective man, though our time together was soon cut short.

Margaret and I were given a pleasant house in a neighbourly area. It was a good place to start my first curacy and here we spent two years, during which time I was made a priest. In the Church of England, one is first made deacon for one year, and then, at a second ordination, one becomes a fully functioning priest. This seem to include being Father Christmas. We also included pilgrimaging (Colour pictures). During my second year as curate Eric departed to Tiverton and I was left monarch of all I surveyed, with the help of a retired priest and one or two 'readers' (lay people trained to conduct some services). I earned my salary (now down to a third of the figure I had earned with the British Council!).

We found time, nevertheless, to welcome our eagerly-awaited third child, Christopher Richard Thompson. It was the time of Enoch Powell's 'rivers of blood' speech. Christopher arrived in Amersham Hospital, in the midst of a circle of nursing staff in the side ward. I looked round and all I could see were white eye-balls and gleaming teeth, revealed in grins of delight.

Each and every one of the maternity staff was black: what should we have done without them?

With the arrival in the parish of the vicar it was time to move on. We had just put on a Holy Week play. The young woman playing Mary Magdalene had actually come to faith on the night of the performance, in that wonderful recognition scene that Luke gives us by the tomb. She is our friend to this day. On the "quit while you are on top" principle, it was time to leave.

I had a hankering to get into work with students. The student chaplaincy work at St Aldate's, Oxford, had been powerful, infectious and fun. It would be good to help build something similar. The Rector of St Aldate's, Canon Keith de Berry, had already given me a nod and a wink that there would be a place for me there in due course. However, at that moment the team was complete. Baulked of St Aldate's, we decided it would only be right to move if a vacancy in student work came up and that was the prayer we prayed. The church paper the next day carried an advertisement from a Liverpool parish involving work with students. It was the Parish of St Matthew and St James, Mossley Hill. It felt right to apply.

The vicar duly met me at the station in his car. As we were driving out of the forecourt he paused for a moment, whereupon the policeman on traffic duty bellowed at him to move on. We were, I realised, no longer in the soft South. Mossley Hill was a distinctly upper crust suburb: the music hall joke was that 'sex' was what you carried coal in up at Mossley Hill. At the turn of the 1900s there had been 20 millionaires in the parish; in my time the score had dwindled to just one – and we took very good care of her. Despite these elevated antecedents, we had our links with popular culture as well! The Beatles had been 'discovered' at a jamboree in the Scout hut and Penny Lane was situated in the parish.

The Sweetwater Canal

"Farewell
Engand"

Our soluble house

The circulating ferry

From gunboat to sailing club HQ

Ordination

Parson's lot

Being Father Christmas

Pilgrim travel

"Hatching"

Salisbury Cathedral

Bath Abbey West Front

"Let there be light"

"The healing of the nations"

Tracksuits – the finished product

Juba School morning assembly

The peace of Galilee

Looking ahead

At that time the parish thought so well of itself that it was deeply mired in an unshakeable complacency. The church's dedication gave the game away. It stood on the crown of a hill, looking down over the leafy acres of Sefton Park ('the Seffy' for Liverpudlians). Its dedication was curious – St Matthew and St James, an unusual coupling. I discovered that the Victorian millionaire who had paid for its construction had modestly dedicated it with his own Christian names. The choir was particularly proud of its achievements and its self-satisfaction was complete when a previous vicar had, on a return visit, declared that "worship at Mossley Hill was near perfection".

I learnt much during my 18 months in the parish, particularly about how not to do things. Throughout my time the vicar was pushing doggedly ahead with his great scheme – to rebuild the church hall. For this he had to carry the members of the Parochial Church Council with him. Their enthusiasm ranged from the half-hearted to the indifferent. One opponent was the treasurer, a former customs officer from Yorkshire with a lifetime's experience of not letting things through. He would listen to the debate about progressing the hall without saying a word until the vicar, with a nervous glance in his direction, would endeavour to call for a vote. Then the treasurer would lumber to his feet and bring progress to a halt with a question – "What I want to know, Mr Chairman, is – where's the money coming from for this 'ere spending spree?"

If some aspects of church life were wearisome, my solace came from the youth club, which was large and lively. On leaving theological college, remembering the problematic experiences of Newquay Grammar School, I had dreaded the prospect of youth work. To my surprise, I had found it easier and far more rewarding to build the informal relationships required in a church youth club than to operate in a disciplinary framework of a school. At Chesham I had even presided over two such clubs – a knockabout affair on a Wednesday for the cheerful unchurched and a more pious group on a Friday called The Young Communicants' Guild.

I remember sitting next to a teenage lass on a Wednesday night session and asking her, in a bellow that just beat the appalling racket of a sound system belting out pop music, what it was that attracted her to the club. I was startled when she told me that she came to the club to get some peace and quiet! I discovered that she came from a family of 17, the despair of the local Social Services. The family was appropriately called Jolly and was housed in two adjacent council houses.

So it was that I came to Mossley Hill's youth work with a degree of optimism – and was not disappointed. The club consisted of a large group of bright, intelligent youngsters who responded well to a challenging programme. I remember leading my confirmation group in a scramble along Helvellyn's Striding Edge, no doubt, in those pre-Health and Safety days, entirely without benefit of appropriate clothing and footwear. One candidate, clinging nervously to a crag, confided in me that he had never realised before that confirmation was so difficult.

Apart from forays up to the Lake District, we took a minibus-load to Wembley to listen to Billy Graham, overnighting happily as guests of the Chesham Young Communicants. The 'Crusade' itself was impressive and brought a number of youngsters to a new level of seriousness in their Christian commitment.

Liverpool itself and our Liverpudlian parishioners presented us with some surprises. The reality of England's north-south divide was brought home to me by the astonishment expressed by some that we should choose for a time to work up north. Liverpool, unlike southern communities, which tend to look to London, had its own life and vigour, which were refreshing. Our youth club would bellow out the Liverpool folk song *We've Got a Cathedral, and Another One to Spare!* With its large Irish population, the Roman Catholic element was very obvious, even without that startlingly successful structure, their conical cathedral, known either as 'Paddy's Wigwam' or 'The Mersey Funnel'. Ecumenical relations, however, were good: as one particularly liberal-minded parishioner put it: "Our neighbours are Catholic but they're very nice"!

I have already mentioned Liverpudlian frankness and outspokenness, which contrast sharply with southern obliqueness and understatement. This northern approach could be bad as well as good. I was particularly incensed by one parishioner who had spoken critically about a young mum whom she believed had left her child unattended while she'd popped out next door for a coffee with a neighbour. Little did she know that the two houses were in fact connected by a baby alarm. Faced with a sermon to the Mother's Union, I resolved to tackle the harm caused by gossip and duly preached on the verse from the Letter of James about the tongue being the rudder of the body. Having delivered myself, I walked to the back of the church and waited, in the spirit of an early Christian martyr, for my fate. My target was a lady well over 6ft tall and broad to match, and she had been known to savage a number of local clergy. She advanced on me and I quailed. Then she took my hand and said: "I'm so glad you preached on that topic: it was very good for them to hear it." The heart of man and woman is desperately deceitful!

In one respect the job fell woefully short of my expectations. I had come to Mossley Hill in the hope of some student chaplaincy work. However, I soon discovered that this was but a twinkle in my vicar's eye, a twinkle he had omitted to share with the duly appointed university chaplain. At that time the university link simply did not happen.

Apart from the difficulties in the work, we had our highlights and our pleasures, with many of our friends coming to visit. We remember the visit of a Brasenose friend, then a lecturer at Liverpool University, who came for tea and stayed for over a month. He was skirting round the edge of a breakdown and was unable to face the stress of lecturing. Helen and Kate might have helped to relieve that stress: our friend would pack them into his car (of all things, it had a sheep's skull on the back shelf, which the girls found extremely exciting!). He would take them to the then abandoned area of the bonded dock warehouses to search for wildflowers. Fortunately, he recovered from his near-breakdown and left university life for what looked like a yet more stressful situation teaching at a boys' public school and made a great success of it. We took the opportunity to get to know new regions – The Isle of Man, southern Ireland, north Wales, and developed a life-long passion for the Lake District.

Liverpool was an important part of our education but offered no long term prospect. Consequently, after 18 months, when an invitation finally came to join the pastorate at St Aldate's, Oxford, it seemed right to accept. There ensued five happy years as Chaplain to the Oxford Pastorate, based at St Aldate's church, and Assistant Chaplain at my old college, Brasenose. The former consisted of caring for a thriving community of 200 or so young students, the latter of conducting the regular services in the college chapel and relating as well as possible to the college community as a whole.

In those days, St Aldate's was its rector, Canon Keith de Berry. Keith, I realised was one of God's good jokes. In some ways he was a conventional, conservative, even Edwardian figure, yet, at the same time, with a great ability for communicating; now in his 60s, he could get through to young men and women in their 20s. Possessing utter conviction in his beliefs, he nonetheless had a sense of humour even about himself. Above all, a messy, untidy, disorganised person who had yet honed up a brilliantly simple system for organising the central strategy of St Aldate's – evangelism.

The first term of the university year, Michaelmas, was devoted to reaching out to the new arrivals in Oxford and if possible winning them for Christ. To this end, all new students, whether nurses, secretarials or undergraduates, were sent an invitation to church on the first Sunday, followed by lunch then or on the succeeding two days. The sermon, given by the rector, was brisk, bright, humorous and evangelistic, the ensuing bunfight a bear garden. Harassed parishioners sought to prepare and serve lunch to an unpredictable number of guests and sometimes 200 a sitting for three days on the trot. After lunch a painfully amateur film was shown about the pastorate's life. The 'catch' from this opening fishing venture was huge and this involved many hours of subsequent interviews and the forming of a number of Beginners' Groups, for those making a fresh or initial beginning in the Christian faith. A further evangelistic preacher was brought in halfway through the term to trawl in any further fish flapping about in the shallows, and the first term's work was consolidated by a weekend residential conference, perhaps 100 strong. The second term built on the first and culminated in two weeks of working parties at Lee Abbey, a former hotel in an idyllic seaside setting on the Devon coast. Now it housed a robust Anglican community, perhaps 100 strong, mainly young. Here students could lock themselves up and read, or else, for a reduced fee, work on the estate. Finally, the third term prepared for the climax of the year – a fortnight's parish mission, where some vicar known to Keith had invited us. The team could be as much as 90 strong.

This year-long flurry of activity was set in motion by a man who was constantly losing his diary and whose correspondence, opened at the breakfast table, often reached the office smeared with marmalade, as Margaret had discovered in those earlier years. The end result of it all, for those who stayed the course, was a constant stream of young men and women whose lives had been liberated and transformed by their encounter with Jesus. Many found their vocation in the ordained ministry.

Working with Keith could be hard work: all such initiators need a team of grey maintainers who can traipse around behind them and pick up the dropped bricks. Yet it was worth it because of the manifest benefits seen in so many lives. It left me with the conviction that, whatever else the ministry might be about, it has to include a concern to let people discover Jesus and grow in his love. St Aldate's showed me that the frustrations of working with Keith paled into insignificance when compared with the results of his labours. He was single-minded and thus highly effective. It was a thrill to work at a church where young undergraduates had to turn up at least 20 minutes early if they were to avoid having to sit on the window sills.

My other work, at Brasenose, moved at a more pedestrian pace but it too had its high points. The pull of Oxford enabled me to invite some distinguished people to preach at evensong. Leonard Cheshire filled the chapel when he described his transition from wartime pilot to committed Christian and founder of the charity homes that bear his name. It was a good moment, too, when the college representative of the University Humanist Society experienced a change of heart and went forward for ordination.

Apart from the chaplaincy, college life offered many delightful moments. Dinner in Hall was a major feature of the whole Brasenose experience. Gowns were worn, allegedly to protect the wearer from careless college servants slopping the soup as they served it, and the meal was prefaced with a long Latin grace, said by a senior scholar. At that time the controversy about admitting women was raging. Only members of the Senior Common Room were allowed to invite female guests; their academic dowdiness was deemed to render them safe from proving a source of temptation to undergraduate eyes.

One evening, however, there was a dramatic change to this pattern. As the dons filed through the doorway behind high table to take their places, it was observed that one guest was a younger lady of surpassing pulchritude – a visiting American professor, it was later discovered. An awe-struck silence gripped the Hall, broken finally by grace, adapted appropriately by the senior scholar – and him a mere scientist at that – so that it started off *"Oculi omnium in te, Dea, spectant..."* ("The eyes of all wait upon thee, O goddess...").

Perhaps the most joyful event of our five years in Oxford was the arrival of our fourth child and second son, Peter Nicholas David. Peter was a joy for us all and Oxford a fabulous place to enjoy family time. Though term-times were incredibly full, the vacations provided time to enjoy camping as a family – often abroad. There was a gospel completeness about four children, two girls and two boys, so we felt the family was now complete.

After these five happy years I was beginning to think it was time for a change of job. The Bishop of Guildford came to preach and stayed to lunch. I made sure I passed him everything he required. The next week I was offered the parish of Ashtead, Surrey, in the Guildford Diocese.

Chapter 10

PARSON'S PLEASURE

The Parish of Ashtead is situated in Surrey, two miles further out of southwest London than Epsom and the first community to lie outside the metropolitan area from which it is separated by the wilderness of Epsom Downs. In my day its population was about 14,000, with two Anglican churches, St Giles and St George's, as well as a Roman Catholic church and a Baptist chapel. St Giles was grey stone, beautiful and ancient, set in parkland next to the old manor house, now the City of London Freeman's School. St George's was modern, red brick and utilitarian, down the hill in Lower Ashtead, the hamlet that had come into being with the construction of the railway line. The whole community was a highly opulent dormitory suburb, just 13 miles from Charing Cross. In my more cynical moments I would claim that it embraced the whole social range from the rich to the stinking rich. Despite its suburban character, I rapidly discovered that there were two words beginning with 's' that if uttered in the pulpit would produce a pin-dropping silence: one was, predictably, 'sex'; the other was 'suburb', if applied to Ashtead, which was firmly designated as a village by its residents.

Church buildings and congregations were well-matched. St Giles's grey stones tended to attract the elderly and the retired, while St George's red brick drew the young-marrieds and the youth. The core of church administration was provided by a nucleus of high calibre civil servants, who were prepared to come, supperless, straight from the London train to an 8.15pm meeting of the Parochial Church Council, which had to conclude by 10.15pm.

Pre-eminent among the civil servants was Edward Smith, a man of genuine humility and utter commitment to the task in hand, whether serving in church or state. ("I have to attend a conference about bananas in Jamaica on Wednesday but I'll be back in time for the Standing and Finance Committee on Friday.") He had interviewed me initially for the post and, after that searching examination, the Last Judgment will be an anti-climax. Once installed, I found his support, as church warden, invaluable; we became good friends. In my time he moved from the Cabinet Office to the Ministry of Agriculture, where, curiously, he carried responsibility for London's flood defences, particularly the Thames Flood Barrier. Once that great piece of engineering was complete and we could all breathe again, recognition was deemed appropriate: at the suggestion of some humourist he was given the Order of the Bath. Sadly, Edward was prone to heart trouble. On one occasion he was due to meet the Queen on two successive days. He did not turn up on the second day: he had died in the night.

Fortunately, for the parish, apart from wonderful lay support, I was buttressed by two curates. One was already in place: Mike Sanders was much loved: with a gentle disposition and the most charismatic of clerical gifts – expertise with the guitar. The other I recruited by telephone. Mark Wilson, to his great credit, agreed to serve in an unvisited parish, with ill-defined duties, living in an unseen house. He proved to be a rock of common sense and good-humoured normality. A dab hand on the cricket field, he was well liked; he and his wife, Mavis, contributed much to the parish. He in due course went on to become an archdeacon, while Mavis was to evolve into a canon of Guildford Cathedral. With two such colleagues, life could not be dull. Being outnumbered prevented my becoming a 'Prince-Rector' and we learned much from each other.

When Mike, after a couple of years, moved on to his own parish, I had to recruit a fresh colleague. I invited a young man, Charles Sherlock, to come and see me. I could not make him out. He seemed a little depressed and quiet, and was clearly not an extrovert: I thought he might find young people difficult. Eventually, I concluded that he would go down well with the elderly and I appointed him. I rapidly found how wrong I had been. He became a kind of Pied Piper for the young, with a knack for exercising gentle care for their spiritual welfare. Other colleagues followed – Peter Wainwright, Patrick Sykes, John Ashe – but I have a particular debt to my first team, who taught me how to be a rector.

It was a good thing our clerical triad enjoyed each other's company, as we had a big job facing us. We had inherited a teeming youth and children's set-up. Attendance at our Sunday morning children's groups numbered well over 600, supervised by 60 group leaders and leading to a 70-strong class each year to be prepared for confirmation. The Moderns' Youth Group then took over, with two meetings a week – Friday night (raucous) and Sunday night after evensong (pious). These after-church meetings were held in the homes of long-suffering parents. I was delighted when, one evening, the crush was so great that a youngster was eased out through the glass of the front door: this, I felt, was New Testament Christianity. The parents in question were less enthused, though we did buy them a new door.

Confirmation was the gateway that admitted to membership of the Moderns, whose popularity thus ensured bumper confirmation groups. The course culminated in a weekend away at a country house conference centre at Ashburnham in Sussex. To get there we used to hire a double-decker bus, rapidly dubbed 'the transport of delight'; all of this added to the attractions of the weekend. The ensuing mix of worship, violent exercise in the pool, an uproarious concert and some straight talking about faith stimulated spiritual progress for many.

It was not just in the area of youth and children's work that I found I had inherited a dynamo. All the parish organisations were in a healthy state, some full of life. The Young Wives had, for reasons of space, to set a limit of 100 members but there were two other women's organisations to accommodate any overflow. Two churches, each with its own ethos, one more conservative and the other open for radical experimentation, enabled large numbers to find a congenial spiritual niche. Our clergy team of three found itself at full stretch but the two curates made excellent role models for the young: each year saw somebody come forward to train for ordination or missionary work overseas. Our problem was to keep up with the congregation and stop them disappearing over the horizon.

Alongside the sometimes frenetic activity of church life ran the normal clergy tasks of hatching, matching and dispatching and, of course, visiting. (Colour picture) Near the rectory lay a group of flats built by an ex-Servicemen's charity for those disabled in the course of their service career. I heard tell of a recently arrived naval commander and went to call on him. I received an effusive welcome: "Delighted to see you, padre. Little woman's away in Kenya visiting family, so there's just me at present. Do come in." I followed him in to his tiny sitting room, where I was startled to see that the whole wall over the fireplace was occupied by an enormous nude, executed in mauve. It was difficult to sustain a conversation with the commander without letting my eyes stray aloft but I did the best I could. As I took my leave, the old sea dog thanked me warmly for calling on him and urged me to call again and meet the little woman after her return. This I duly did some weeks later and was again cordially welcomed, this time by the two of them. As we entered the sitting room, my gaze stole to the space above the fireplace: it was occupied by a small sepia print of Durham Cathedral. My eyes met those of the commander and a look of purest understanding passed between us.

Our 11 years at Ashtead were perhaps among our happiest: we had been made so welcome and made many friends. It was where our four children grew up in our delightful rectory. Margaret's role was strenuous but she rose to the challenge. Making up 200 yards of curtaining for the rectory on arrival was her baptism of fire. Thereafter she involved herself busily in the life of our women's organisations. Only once did her touch fail. I had asked her to stand outside St George's to welcome the bishop and his wife when he came to conduct our confirmation service. It was obvious on their arrival that all was not well with the episcopal pair: a certain air of tension suggested there had been words along the way. The bishop, slightly late, alighted briskly and said to his wife: "Get my robes case out of the boot, please." "There's no case here: you know with my back I can't be lifting cases." "But, I asked you..." The parents flocking into church were clearly enjoying this heated discussion, so Margaret felt called to intervene and cool it. "Don't worry, there are plenty of robes in the vestry and we can find something suitable." Then, hoping to pour the oil of humour on to troubled waters, she added: "And if it's a mitre you need, I can always pop home and get the tea cosy." "What nonsense!" snorted the bishop and, taking his wife's arm, led the way into church, the two of them reunited by their joint indignation.

A happier visitor occasion occurred soon after our arrival. The phone rang and a voice said: "I am Cliff Richard's agent: now, about his visit next month..." My predecessor had entirely failed to mention to me this long-standing invitation. We went into top gear and, in due course, the great star arrived. He came to tea, first at the rectory (a particular type of biscuit is still known in the family as a Cliff Richard biscuit and duly revered). By pure chance our elder daughter, Helen, was elected to travel in Cliff's sports car to show him the way to St George's. It was a great evening and it did us all good to see a queue winding round the parish church beforehand.

After 10 years I and the parish were both exhausted and it was time to think of moving on. I had received great stimulus by being invited to attend, some years previously, a month-long Mid-service Clergy Course, held in the slightly surreal, *Alice In Wonderland*, surroundings of Windsor Castle. Now something similar was needed to make possible some reflection on where to go next. I had heard of a similar course held in the States, at the Episcopalian seminary at Alexandria, just outside Washington DC and I duly wrote for details. To my amazement I received a letter by return offering me the annual Commonwealth scholarship, which would pay all fees, leaving just the airfare to find. "But, especially in this horrible, snowy weather, I can't leave you to cope for a month," I protested to Margaret. "Shut up and go," she replied, so I went. As a *quid pro quo* she received a new kitten, which, of course, was given the name Washington.

As I had never before crossed the Atlantic, this was a great adventure. At Dulles Airport the immigration officer was a black man. On seeing my passport, a great beam spread across his face. Extending his hand he said: "Put it there, Mr Askew, my name's Askew too". I at once felt welcomed and at home, even though I subsequently discovered that our shared surname probably meant that he had a slave-ancestor working for some 18th century Askew.

The seminary is set in beautiful parkland next to the pleasant town of Alexandria, 10 miles out of Washington. My Brasenose friend, Gerry Dunphy, put me up on arrival but I then moved into the Seminary's Continuing Education block, where I had a comfortable bed-sit. My 12 companions on the course were all American clergy, most of them Episcopalian. The course was wide rather than deep and catered for the whole person, rather than Windsor's more cerebral approach. The programme included a number of excursions. An early visit to Washington to see a Rodin exhibition, on a day of blizzards and foot-deep snow, coincided with the ghastly tragedy of an Air Florida airliner, with 79 on board, taking off with wings not properly de-iced, touching the rail on the bridge over the Potomac and plunging into the icy river: only five survived.

Despite this sad start, I retain warm memories of good friends and horizon-widening tales, despite some zany elements in our syllabus (the "Male Consciousness-Raising Workshop" was particularly testing for anyone born south of the Watford Gap). One module invited us to list all our triumphant achievements since age two so as to assist in finding our next career step. I had always thought this would be vouchsafed to me on my knees, when guidance would be lowered on a golden thread from heaven. This was not the seminary-encouraged strategy. "Use mail-shots to bishops," we were urged.

I returned from Washington in a mood of divine impatience, only to be brought down to earth by Margaret's asking why I was so irritable. I unveiled to her the new doctrine of episcopal mail-shots. But whom could we 'shoot'? While at St Aldate's I had felt that some further study of theology might be helpful in such an academic atmosphere, so I had signed up for the Oxford Diploma in Theology, with the Chaplain of Corpus Christi, John Austin Baker, as my tutor. He had now just been elevated to become Bishop of Salisbury and, greatly daring, I wrote to him asking for a job. He was so surprised at my audacity that he invited me for interview for the post of Diocesan Missioner, fortuitously vacant.

On the appointed day, Margaret and I drove nervously into Salisbury's vast Cathedral Close and up to the Bishop's Palace at South Canonry. An embarrassed secretary said the bishop was still out; would we come back in an hour? We did, only to meet the same request. Eventually we got to meet a tired bishop, who had been in court all day defending the Greenham Common women's anti-nuclear demonstration. On the basis of a 20 minute interview I was offered the post. "I'm afraid," said the Bishop, apologetically, "if we are to give you a house and a salary I shall have to ask you to become Canon Treasurer of the cathedral as well." Magnanimously, I agreed to carry this extra burden and was duly appointed as Diocesan Adviser on Mission and Ministry and Canon Treasurer of Salisbury Cathedral. (Colour picture)

Alongside this unexpected elevation to the ecclesiastical stratosphere, Margaret, too, had been blossoming and flourishing. She had taken a Mothers' Union course while we were at Ashtead that must have come just at the right time for her. It was ostensibly about training up Mothers' Union speakers but had, for her, a powerfully liberating effect. She was emboldened to train as an Adult Education Teacher, to teach crafts, and gained teaching experience in various craft centres and care homes.

Chapter 11

GOD ON HIGH AND GOD IN THE MIDST

The theologians tell us that God is to be experienced in two contrasting ways: we may either encounter Him in His transcendence – up, out there – or meet Him in His immanence – here, now, among us. We had been very aware of Him at the Ashtead end of the spectrum as 'God-in-the-midst' (sometimes prompting a debased form of worship known as 'being matey with the Almighty'). We were now plucked out of this pleasant and companionable soup of immanence and plunged into a cold douche of transcendence. Salisbury's majestic spire is the highest in England and inevitably dictates the attitudes of those who say their prayers beneath it. Here is God 'high and lifted up' and we are cowed almost into insignificance in His presence. Inevitably, worship is formed and can degenerate into being depersonalised and remote. The contrast with our farewell send-off at St George's, Ashtead, with a couple of hundred people joining hands to sing *Bind us together, Lord* could hardly have been more acute. We found ourselves emotionally cast up, high and dry, especially Margaret, who had surrendered her role as rector's wife, with its involvement in parish life, and was now separated from a great many friends. I, at least, had my work: she had to find hers. She triumphantly succeeded in this by developing the use of our medieval cellar for giving adult education craft classes and participated also in teaching on a Youth Training Scheme.

In theory, I was to divide my time equally between cathedral and diocese. In practice, any such 50-50 division can become, unless you are careful, 100-100. My first move, therefore, was to dream up a cathedral job description, limiting my role, and to get it signed by bishop and dean. In reality, I was much more attracted to the diocesan task than to the cathedral. The former was mobile, dynamic and whizzy: the latter was static, geriatric and conservative. As the least musical clergyman in the Church of England, the cathedral's finest achievement – its choral tradition – was largely lost on me, though for Margaret, on the other hand, it was a great enrichment: for the rest, although the cathedral's architecture and setting were magnificent, its congregational life at that time did not greatly impress me. We were able to notch up some successes in humanising the cathedral. Margaret was the intrepid pioneer who trail-blazed coffee after the Eucharist. There were dire predictions about dumbing down the worship by reducing the service to a church meeting but she persevered. When the great Coffee Day came, contrary to alarmist fears, the roof did not collapse – although perhaps a few cobwebs were shaken down.

In the diocese, I had inherited a rag-bag of functions grouped under a majestic title – Adviser on Mission and Ministry. Here I had an office and a secretary, and I sat on various committees dealing with different aspects of the work, which in practice covered lay theological education (there was a course in theology for lay people known as the Bishop's Certificate course); lay training – we were trying to develop a ministry of what were to be called Lay Pastoral Assistants; the production each year of a diocesan Lent course, to be used in home groups across the diocese; the encouragement of any evangelistic initiatives that might appear; support for our longstanding diocesan link with the Episcopal Church of the Sudan; and anything else that might be dreamed up to mobilise the diocese. It was a tall order.

The Bishop's Certificate course, I discovered, was due for rewriting. Over two years a committee of six achieved this and, eventually, we had 200 students beavering away in tutor groups for six 'terms'. Each summer we had a gathering one Saturday with some well-known visiting speaker from beyond the diocese and a 'prizegiving'.

The Lay Pastoral Assistants' course was but a twinkle in the Bishop's eye. I turned the twinkle into paper and produced a skeletal course that could bring the congregation's practical good neighbours into ministry. The Lent course meant the writing of a fresh, six-session booklet each year and the home-grown printing of it in Church House. The work was based in a delightful and historic building on the banks of the River Avon (an early owner had been beheaded for treason). In the early 19th century it had been bought up and turned into the Church of England's first diocesan office by a felicitously named cleric – Archdeacon Sanctuary (are people's careers often dictated by their surnames?)

As for the Sudan, our previous experience of that country was useful. I was put on the Sudan committee and, to our joy, we were both sent out to represent the diocese at the triumphant consecration of not one but five bishops (see Chapter 14). Finally, much time was devoted to an initiative entitled Going for Goals, which sought to employ the strategy of 'management by objectives' in the service of parochial church councils. First of all, we produced a home-made comic-strip booklet, together with a tape-slide programme, contrasting the mythical practices of the United Benefice of Much Dithering with Little Doing with the achievements of some actual well-organised parishes. Armed with this powerful weapon, I would sally out to PCCs that asked for a presentation, from north Wiltshire to west Dorset. I would then show the slides and challenge them to draw themselves up a one-year plan. Surprisingly, this campaign proved popular with the parishes, if exhausting for me, as I had to tote the antiquated technology round the diocese two or three evenings a week (nowadays it would be DVDs and Powerpoint; then it was a slide projector and a tape recorder). Nevertheless, though viewed coolly by my episcopal masters, it did have a bracing and stimulating effect in the parishes, bringing numerous parish projects to pass.

The diocesan commitment was a man-eater, moving ahead at a much faster pace than the Trollopian amble of the Cathedral Close. Living in the Close was seductive, if a touch unreal. Many of the houses had ancient origins, disguised by a triumphant face-lift carried out to celebrate the return of the monarchy in 1660 after the Civil War. Our house, Loders, at the end of Rosemary Lane, was a delight, with a charming garden backed up against the wall surrounding the Close. It had a 13th century cellar with a staircase to nowhere disappearing into the ceiling. Our family loved the place and saw the cellar as the perfect venue for parties and multi-decibel music that rocked the foundations. I lived in daily anticipation of complaints from the neighbouring pub, giving rise to banner headlines of the Man Bites Dog type in the Salisbury Journal... 'Pub Deafened By Canon's Cacophony'.

It was in the cellar here that Margaret carried through her vast tracksuit project (see Chapter 14). Suffice to say that I remain the only Canon of Salisbury Cathedral who has had six miles of knicker elastic delivered to the Close, permanently lowering its tone.

There were two other significant ramifications of my work as Adviser on Mission and Ministry. Because I was well known in the diocese I was elected to the General Synod, the Church's central 'parliament': and I also went on to become involved in the selection procedure for those seeking to be ordained.

General Synod met three times a year, twice in London and once in York. Its London base was Church House, Westminster, a few hundred yards away from the House of Commons. It was not always beneficial to be so much in the shadow of our parliamentary 'Big Brother'. There was a tendency to accentuate matters of procedure and even, perhaps, degrees of pomposity. However, our debates could draw upon a wide circle of expertise and even at times provide a higher level of discussion than was possible in the politicised House across the way. This was never more apparent than in the historic debate on the nuclear bomb, which was well conducted in the glare of the TV lights. Most of the time, however, we were engaged in more pedestrian matters, such as setting the level for wedding fees and deciding policy about bats in the belfry (yes, really!). The overarching Church question of the time was the ordination of women, which had already been on the agenda for 10 years or so. Eventually, however, the women's silent picketing of every session had its effect and a decisive vote enabled women to be ordained priests at last and to enjoy a long-overdue victory. Over the coming months 400 clergy left the Church of England (though 200 or so returned later); in time 1,200 women were ordained to take their places and swell our ranks.

The breadth of experience in the Synod was clearly revealed in one debate, about the governing of cathedrals. Cathedrals were then an 18th century anomaly, in that the dean had no clear authority over his team of three or four canons, who were appointed for life. At Lincoln, in particular, the matter had reached scandal pitch, as the canons were at loggerheads with the dean and refused even to attend a weekly staff meeting.

Affairs at Lincoln, therefore, lay behind the debate, though nobody had so far mentioned that cathedral at that point. Then a tall, bearded man rose to speak. In a loud voice he declared: "Matters at Lincoln will never be resolved until the participants fall within my jurisdiction." Sensation! People craned their heads to see who this stranger was. His next words resolved the question: "I am the Coroner of Lincoln".

If General Synod had its moments of farce, as well as much tedium, the clergy selection procedure, on the other hand, was both strenuous and absorbing. Candidates were invited for a three-day conference at some diocesan retreat centre. Here four examiners, both clerical and lay, would interview each candidate, one to one, from different viewpoints – pastoral, academic and so on. Voluminous references on each had to be read up in advance. Brief addresses had to be delivered by each candidate on a subject of their choice. Finally, after the candidates had departed, there took place 'the night of the long knives', where the examiners met to dissect their victims. The system seems well-nigh infallible and yet nonetheless some peculiar people do get through the net. When taxed about some clerics' shortcomings, I am accustomed to answer: "It's not surprising we have some disappointments amongst the clergy. The field for selection is very limited. There's only you lay people to choose us from."

Among the big events that took place during my time as Canon Treasurer, I think of three in particular – a memorial service; a royal visit; and an encounter with a group of Russian visitors. The memorial service was held on a lovely day of high summer. A London policewoman, WPC Yvonne Fletcher, had been shot dead from inside the Libyan Embassy while controlling a crowd protesting outside the building. Her killer was clearly a member of the embassy staff. His motive was unclear but, though the man was known to the police, he was able to depart after some days, under the cloak of diplomatic immunity. Yvonne came from Wiltshire, so it was natural to make use of Salisbury Cathedral for the memorial service. The church was packed out with her fellow officers from the Metropolitan Police, many of them reduced to tears before the end of the service. Bishop John Baker preached very sensitively. It was the service that, for me, was outstanding in its sincerity and emotional intensity.

The Royal visit was paid by Prince Charles, who came to inaugurate the Save Our Spire appeal, which was looking for £16 million. Again, it was a lovely day. He was to arrive by helicopter and had chosen to fly it himself. Dead on the dot, the vast, blood-red machine touched down by the West Front. The Prince climbed down, ran a comb through his hair and plunged into the service. His role was to read the lesson – from the Authorised Version, of course.

The other visit came towards the end of my time, at the start of *glasnost*. Amazingly, an early exchange brought a group of Russian scientists from their chemical warfare establishment to our chemical defence establishment at Porton Down. I knew one of our top scientists there and he was in charge of arranging the programme for their leisure evening. "Would they like a tour of the cathedral?" I asked. He jumped at the idea and on the appointed day Margaret and I waited in the Close for the arrival of a luxury coach. Out climbed 20 or so baggy-flannelled scientists; an equal number of our own boffins; a contingent from the Russian Embassy to ensure that nothing untoward was said; the Russian Ambassador to the current disarmament talks and ours to match him; and a very worried young naval sub-lieutenant clutching an enormous dictionary; he asked us plaintively to tip him off before embarking on any ecclesiastical terms. The whole event had escalated from our original plan. The evening was a great success: we started off with the Chapter House and Magna Carta ("the basis of our civil liberties") and ended up in the Amnesty International Chapel, where, fortunately, the specially remembered prisoner of the month was not from the USSR! Afterwards, we strolled across to our rather magnificent house, which I passed off as standard clergy accommodation. Thereafter, the conversation and the vodka ran, for the most part, freely: there was one sticky moment when I asked one of the scientists to explain *glasnost*: "Oh," he answered nervously, "It's purely an economic movement."

At the end, the commandant made a little speech of thanks. I had to reply – and inspiration struck! I gave them Lermontov's poem on freedom, without ever revealing that I had learnt it in preparation for joining the Intelligence Corps to spy on Russian radio signals. When I had finished, there was hardly a dry eye in the room.

"Quit while you're on top," I thought. "It's time to move on from Salisbury's lush Close and comfortable stall." I had been there for seven years, and seven is the biblical number for completeness. It was definitely time to go.

Chapter 12

THE LANTERN OF THE WEST

Once again we were on the move and up for offers. At the start of the process I had said grumpily to Margaret: "One thing is certain. Our next church is not going to be a great pile of stone with a high musical tradition and a massive financial appeal hanging over it." It is said that 'If you want to make God laugh, tell him your plans.'

When it became known that I was looking to move, an approach was made to me to consider becoming Rector of Bath Abbey. My only previous acquaintance with the church had come when, as a parent, I had attended the Abbey for the Monkton Combe School Carol Service, as our two boys were attending the school. I had not been impressed: the building was cold and soot-stained (it had been gas-lit until 1978) and the sound amplification was poor – altogether not a good welcome for the school. I found that the rector had been in the post for 30 years, thus defining the Christian ministry for all time. Naturally, the congregation had become a little bit stuck. Once again the choral tradition seemed its best point, much of it lost on me: and, yes, there was a financial appeal pending. Nevertheless the Bishop of Bath and Wells, George Carey, was anxious for me to look at the vacancy. With a heavy heart we drove across to meet the two parish representatives who were to conduct the interview; I had discovered that I was candidate number eight, the previous seven having declined or been rejected. It was not a happy evening. The representatives had clearly been briefed to be wary of change and to ensure the continuance of a rather conservative pattern of church life. I reacted somewhat perversely to their probing and was vastly relieved to receive a letter from the parish representative two days later advising me not to proceed.

However, that was not the end of the matter. Some weeks later I was approached again by Bishop Carey while up at General Synod and asked to reconsider. By now time had run out for the Abbey's appointment: the parishioners had lost the right to reject candidates and were now obliged to accept whoever the bishop might send to them. However, I did not like the idea of being put in against the wishes of the PCC, so I suggested a compromise. I would be prepared to meet the PCC and explain my position, provided I could present my views and they could have a chance to express their opinion. By now I was candidate number 11. I wrote a careful address, setting out my 'manifesto', saying what changes I would want to make, if appointed. The evening came; I said my piece and at once departed. No questions were permitted. "That," I thought, "has sealed off Bath Abbey and I can get on with a real search." Imagine my chagrin when, next morning, an exultant archdeacon rang to tell me the PCC members had approved of my paper 22 to six. With a heavy heart I accepted my destiny and agreed to become Rector of Bath Abbey. (Colour picture)

The Abbey, despite its exalted title, was in fact a parish church, albeit a large one. It had had a chequered history. The site on which it stood, on a high bluff overlooking the river Avon, had been considered numinous ever since the days of the aboriginal Celts, who were awe-struck by the springs of hot water that burst out of the ground here. They had decided this phenomenon must be a sign of divine favour, so they built a temple to their goddess Sul. When the Romans invaded in AD 43 their first move was to put their oppressive stamp on the place by driving a road through the Celtic temple precinct. Later on, perhaps chastened by Boudicca's revolt, wiser counsels prevailed and they adopted the site, twinning Sul with their own goddess Minerva and tactfully naming the settlement *Aquae Sulis*. The archaeologists trace two Roman temples – one dedicated to Sul Minerva and the other, facing it across a sacred courtyard, a circular structure beneath the spot where hymn books are now handed out, at the back of the Abbey nave. Time passed. Saxons succeeded Romans, but not before Christianity had arrived in the city, round about AD 200. A prayer to Minerva was once scratched on to a piece of lead, as was the custom: this was then rolled up and thrown into the Great Bath, where it remained in peace until discovered, unrolled and deciphered in the 1970s: it proved to be a curse written by one Annianus on whoever "whether pagan or Christian" had pinched the author's six pieces of silver. So our spiritual ancestors, whether or not honest, had a toehold in Bath as early as the late AD 300s. The Saxon invaders were also Christian, and, in AD 675, an intrepid community of nuns had established themselves, probably where the Abbey now stands. A century later they were succeeded by monks, 'the brothers of St Peter', anticipating the church's present dedication to St Peter and St Paul. A crude cathedral took shape and in time a saintly figure became abbot of the monastery: his name was Alphege. He went on to become Archbishop of Canterbury. Kidnapped by the Vikings, he was martyred in AD 1012 for refusing to pass on their ransom demands to the impoverished farmers of Kent.

Then came 1066 and all that. The triumphant Normans knocked down the primitive cathedral and built a better one in its place. This survived for two centuries, when a fire necessitated a second rebuild. The present church stands within the outline of its nave, while its great apse once occupied the Orange Grove roundabout in the east. Sadly, the monastery dwindled in numbers and the building was allowed to fall into disrepair. In 1499 a new broom bishop came up from Wells (whither the diocesan centre had been removed), decreed the destruction of the derelict structure, inflicted financial penalties on the monks and ordered the building of the present church, in the Perpendicular style he knew from his time at Eton and King's, Cambridge. Thus the last great medieval church came into being, just in time to be closed down in 1538 by a money-hungry Henry VIII, with his eye on the monastic endowments.

For nearly a century the building lay unfinished, for nobody wanted to pick up the tab for completing it. The local MP, Sir John Harington (eponymously remembered as the inventor of the water closet, or 'John'), invited Bishop Montague from Wells to view the sorry state of affairs. It was pouring with rain but, as they stood in the still-unroofed nave, they continued to get wet. "Sire," said the astute MP, "if this building cannot save us from the waters above, how will it save us from the fires below?" The bishop got the message and duly paid to have the nave roofed, while his brother, a judge, provided the great west doors. Following a visit by Queen Elizabeth I in 1574 and a royal tantrum over the scandal of the unfinished church, some local worthies at last paid up and the building was reopened as a parish church in 1616. It acquired its nickname, 'The Lantern of The West', because of its vast area of plain glass windows, the church having been closed down by Henry VIII's commissioners before coloured glass could be installed. (Colour picture)

There followed the religious dissensions of the 17th century and the bitter conflicts of the Civil War (the Abbey was for a time a military hospital). The next century saw Bath's architectural renaissance after its previous squalor. (At the time of Elizabeth I's visit, the widest street, Cheap Street, was just 6ft wide). With the rebuilding came Beau Nash and his development of the city's social life to make it a leisured Mecca where the wealthy classes could spend their summers: the Abbey was one of the hubs of his regulated programme.

Bath waned somewhat in the 19th century, as coastal resorts such as Brighton proved to be counter-attractions. But the city's new population of retirees continued to flock to the Abbey's matins in their bathchairs. The past century saw the traumas of two world wars and two nights of bombing on undefended Bath in 1942; the Abbey's east window was blown in by a bomb that fell a few hundred yards away in the recreation ground. After the war came a costly refurbishment of the Abbey in the incumbency of Archdeacon Selwyn. When I came on the scene, a second such programme, to deal with the West Front, was becoming due.

It is necessary at this point to make an excursus to underline the fact that taking on the Abbey meant assuming a burden of history and conservative expectations. It was with a heavy heart that I prepared to undertake what I assumed would be an attempt to make a juggernaut oil tanker change course. At Salisbury my predecessor in the role of treasurer was a saint, St Edmund Rich. At Bath, St Alphege lurked in the background. How can one cope with being surrounded by such an embarrassing cloud of witnesses? I was about to find out.

Chapter 13

AT SATAN'S THRONE

A frequent 18th century visitor to Bath was John Wesley. He came not because he liked the city but because he feared for it. He strongly disapproved of the card-playing, drinking, dancing and womanising that accompanied the leisured regime of Bath's visitors. At the back of it all stood the local council-appointed master of ceremonies, Beau Nash, and Wesley identified Nash as the cause of everything he deplored about the city. His name for Bath was 'Satan's Throne' and there was no doubt who occupied the title role.

The story is told that Nash and Wesley once found themselves face to face on the pavement: one of them was going to have to step off into the mud and filth of the roadway. "I never give way to fools and blackguards," growled Nash: "But I always do," muttered Wesley and meekly stepped into the slush.

So, here I was in charge of the building that bore on its walls Beau Nash's epitaph, couched in the respectability of the Latin tongue. The Abbey latterly had settled into a maintenance-only rut, from which not even the triumph of Easter Day and other festivals could lift it. Easter Day came soon after my arrival and I determined to mark it properly. Accordingly, I ordered a flamboyant 'Jesus Lives!' poster, set it on an easel outside the west door and went off on my post-Easter break. I returned to find that an over-zealous defender of the *ancien régime* had taken my easel and poster and hurled them in fury down into the moat surrounding the church! Next year, I promised myself, it would be different.

Our bishop always visited the Abbey to preach at matins at Christmas and Easter. When next Easter came round, we turned the occasion into a demo. Choosing the longest hymn in the book as the final hymn, we arranged for the congregation to be led out singing into the square that faced our West Front. Holidaymakers drinking their coffee at the pavement café choked as they watched the choir-led congregation of 1,200 debouching into the open space. Meanwhile, the clergy and bishop climbed to the West Front gallery, where the bishop was given three minutes to explain Easter before pronouncing his blessing *urbi et orbi* (to the city and the world). From that day on it was seen that Easter was different from other Sundays. The annual demo, later embellished by trumpet fanfares, was accepted and appreciated.

The biggest challenge confronting the Abbey was, inevitably, concerned with the fabric and the cash to repair it. Plans had already been launched to refurbish the West Front, with its magnificent array of statues – the good and great flanked by the angels, who were ascending and descending two ladders: I urged the Church Council not to proceed straight away but instead to reflect on what else needed to be done before launching a campaign to raise the total sum needed. Eventually we identified six major projects: to carry through the work on the West Front: to relight the interior; to clean the interior walls and ceiling; to rebuild the organ; to build an underground museum in the vaults on the Abbey's south side; and to clean as much of the rest of the exterior as we could. I worked out the cost on the back of an old envelope and wrote down £2½ million: in fact we ceased fundraising when we reached £4 million.

Our task was firstly to strengthen the life of the congregation and, secondly, to use the Abbey's situation as the most visited parish church in the country (first equal with St Mary the Virgin,

Oxford) to proclaim the faith in whatever ways were appropriate. With the congregation, the main need was to promote the Abbey as a participatory parish church and not like a cathedral where it is possible to pop in from time to time. We wanted people to belong and not just to attend. Our best stratagem here was achieved entirely by chance and without our realising the results. There was already a body of stewards, to welcome and inform our crowds of visitors: to this we added two further groups – one to run the new bookshop (Margaret was one of the leadership team): another, in due course, to steward the under-ground Heritage Vaults museum. Each team was about 60 strong and people would operate in pairs or triplets. The result was a massive 'getting to know you' with unintended but beneficial effects by which Abbey members acquired one or two close colleagues whom they had probably not met before.

Our second, more conscious, initiative was to expand greatly all forms of lay ministry, which previously had been kept within the iron grasp of the clergy – lesson reading, leading home groups, conducting intercessions, training as pastoral assistants. This development was in due course accelerated by running an Alpha course and by our pilgrimages, of which more later.

To my surprise, I found these good developments were actually encouraged by the massive fundraising campaigning necessitated by the fabric work. 'Bath Abbey 2000' was managed by a fundraiser seconded from a specialist fundraising firm; Ken Pearson, who proved to be both congenial and Christian. His first move was to address the Parochial Church Council on 'Fundraising Today'. In no time at all he had a bemused council, who had thought they were to hear an academic talk on the theology of fundraising, enrolled as a fundraising team; each one was charged with approaching half a dozen members of the congregation (after, of course, making their own pledge). The results were dynamic: to engage our specialist firm, we had had to make a large down-payment, with no certainty of recouping it. Yet, within days, the Church Council were bringing in generous pledges that easily topped this down-payment. In all, the congregation was to raise a quarter of a million pounds, which enabled us, when approaching charities and other bodies, to look them in the eye.

In another way, too, Bath Abbey 2000 gave us a much-needed stimulus. On my arrival the Abbey's secretarial back-up consisted of one lady using her own typewriter at home. The Abbey owned a small house immediately adjacent to it but this was used only for storing the stage required for concerts. Under the impulse of the campaign, this house was repaired, the stage removed, two secretaries employed and computers, telephones, a photocopier and a fax machine installed. The Abbey now had an administrative heart.

The only component of the work to be done that was entirely new was the creation of the museum in the vaults alongside the Abbey, which had once been the coal cellars of the cottages huddled there. The construction of the museum was an idea we were keen to carry out: we felt there was a Christian story to tell and, in a city teeming with both visitors and museums, this was the right way to tell it. We held a meeting of those interested in the project down in the vaults. The work was, of course, behind schedule, so when we met there was no electricity and the roof dripped water. I thought we should never see the volunteers again: in fact, they all turned up when the The Vaults opened for our visitors.

The area of the vaults lay over the cloisters that had been the old monastic burial ground. The local archaeologists got very excited and insisted on excavating no less than 30 skeletons.

114

The first one to be dug up turned out to be that of a woman, a fact which led to a certain amount of ribald speculation among the vergers. Actually, she must have been a wealthy benefactress to be accorded this privilege. All the skeletons, after being carbon-dated at Bristol, were returned for burial: this proved to be the occasion of a very positive ecumenical service shared with the monks of Downside Abbey, at which we reburied the skeletal remains.

As the works proceeded the congregation had the satisfaction of seeing immediate results, with successive completions, switch-ons, openings or blessings. Alongside the practical work we promoted the idea that the congregation also should be spiritually renewed to match the refurbishment of the fabric.

It was my hope that an ordinand would emerge from among us to encourage us all. We nearly managed it. A young widow seemed eminently qualified. She had a first class degree and a responsible post in the library service. She rang the bells, served on the PCC and had ploughed in her experience of widowhood by working for the Cruse charity. Wonderfully, she went forward for selection. This meant, first, an interview with the Bishop's Examining Chaplain and then, if he approved, referral on to a national selection conference. She duly went off for a lengthy interview with the chaplain, was sent on to the selection conference, but was then unaccountably not recommended for training. I was extremely puzzled until two weeks later, when the mystery was resolved: her engagement was announced – to the Bishop's Examining Chaplain, whom she had met for the first time in her interview. They were married in the Abbey by the bishop, who, in his address, said this gave an entirely new take on the phrase "Bishop's Examining Chaplain"!

Over the years we saw a freeing up of the congregation and a greater willingness to get involved, and this was helped rather than hindered by Bath Abbey 2000. But there was also the Abbey's external ministry to our visitors (300,000 *per annum*) and to the city of Bath. As regards the visitors, the first year had been devoted to improving the immediate impression the Abbey gave. "No" notices, lots of them, were summarily removed. Then we refined the excellent leaflet left by my predecessor and given to all visitors. It presented a summary of Christian belief in a couple of pages, and a guide round the church. We had it translated into more languages (an early Russian visitor, impressed, took one home, unknown to us, and sent us a translation). The chapels at the east end were opened for prayer and suitable prayer material supplied. Margaret launched the inspired notion of a chapel devoted to St Alphege (once prior to the monastic community and later to become Archbishop of Canterbury) and the Friends of Bath Abbey brought it into being. They also paid for some magnificent and arresting frontals erected by Jane Lemon of Salisbury and her Sarum Group of embroiderers. On the south side of the High Altar, balancing Alphege on the north, an old choir vestry became the Gesthemane Chapel, with perhaps the finest frontal of all. A video, *Easter People*, was made and played on a loop during visitor hours to show that the Abbey was people as well as stones. A corps of retired clergy was recruited to be on duty in the Abbey, chat to visitors, and lead hourly prayers. Inevitably they were soon known as 'Dad's Army'. In all, any visitor could not help feeling welcomed; being given a chance to learn something about Christian belief and being encouraged to pray.

Early on I came to realise the width of the Abbey's parish boundaries when I received a letter from Springfield, Missouri, taking up a point I had made in my sermon two Sundays previously. There were normally 20 to 30 overseas visitors each Sunday morning. We hosted the annual Civic Service and the

University's degree ceremony (with some reluctance they permitted us to open it with a prayer). Among a plethora of school carol services there was a notable one provided by the Bath Chronicle for its readers: the order of service was printed as an inset in the paper and it was fascinating to look at a congregation with its noses buried in their newspapers!

The approach of the Millennium gave us the opportunity to carry forward one or two plans. The decline of work with young people has been the saddest aspect of the Church of England in recent decades and the Abbey was no exception. Yet, with a strong boys' choir and now a girls' choir to join it, we were in touch with a lot of youngsters. So we set ourselves to raise money to appoint a youth leader for three years. Our appointee was tough (she had played rugby for Bath City Women's XV!) and highly effective. Then we asked the Friends if they would commission a statue of the Risen Lord to stand outside the Abbey and they employed the talent of a local sculptor, Lawrence Tindall, to good effect. Finally, we instituted an annual Wilberforce lecture to be delivered on any subject reflecting 'the application of Christian principles to public life'.

Many of our plans came to fruition by 2000. Bath Abbey 2000 was done and dusted and the Prince of Wales, our patron, visited to sign it off. Our three Millennium projects had all come to pass. I was looking forward to retirement, perhaps in 2001.

One day in 1999 I visited a parishioner in an office block close to the Abbey. I bounded up the five flights of stairs and congratulated myself on not feeling puffed. But that evening in the bath I felt ominous pains in chest and arms. A spell in hospital ensued, with an angioplasty procedure. It was a warning and we heeded it, bringing forward my retirement to June 2000 and sealing off 10 unexpectedly happy and creative years. My last parish commitment was to preside over the first Wilberforce lecture, delivered by Bath's former MP, Chris Patten. Having arrived in Bath with feelings approaching dread, we left with gratitude, regret and many friends.

Chapter 14

FOREIGN AFFAIRS

Prime Minister Herbert Asquith was once asked about King Edward VII, after the success of his Paris visit in establishing an *entente cordiale* with France: "Would it be right to entrust the King with a definite role in Foreign Affairs?" Asquith shook his head decisively. "Foreign Affairs – never! Affairs with foreigners – certainly."

I have been rather more fortunate than Edward VII, in that my career has embraced a number of precious and rewarding overseas commitments. On a more peaceful note, the course at the Alexandria Seminary in the USA, already mentioned in Chapter 10, was invaluable in widening horizons and revealing a Church situation that was both positive and confident. The dozen other clergy I met there (all Americans) proved to be good friends. On the second day, when hearing my English accent, one said: "It's all right, Richard. We don't mind about your speech 'defect'!" After that, I knew I was in. Most of the group subsequently visited us in Salisbury, either in person or vicariously through their backpacking offspring. It must be said, however, with regard to the college's recommended formula for finding another post – mailshots to bishops – only in my case did it appear to have worked! It lifted me from a hyper-active commuting suburb to the sublime seclusion of Salisbury Cathedral. The American system had proved too exhaustive and too expensive for the Americans themselves!

My time at Ashtead coincided with the grimmest period of Ireland's "troubles". It was the time of internment, hunger strikes and suicides, and bomb atrocities on both sides of the

Irish Channel. As we enjoyed good relations with our Roman Catholic neighbour in Ashtead, and as the parish as a whole deplored the bloodshed and wished to offer constructive help, we planned an ecumenical venture: we set up a couple of holiday schemes by which Belfast children of the two communities could visit Ashtead and share a couple of weeks of activities in a way that would have been impossible back home.

As a preparation, the Roman Catholic priest and I flew to Belfast to meet the children and the parishioners. It was uncanny to discover how just a few miles of sea separated us from a situation so utterly different from our own. Instead of the peace of Ashtead's leafy avenues, we were confronted by Army patrols, barbed wire and numerous checkpoints manned by armed police. On my first day I was taken on a 'tour of the battlefield'. We paused for lunch at a pub protected against bombing by bollards five yards out into the pavement. The door was locked and only inspection through an eyehole permitted us to enter. Once inside, I put down my bag with relief and sauntered across to the bar to order something to eat. I was aware of a commotion behind me but paid no attention. Only when I turned round did I see that the presence of my bag on the floor had precipitated a panic rush to the other end of the room. I felt duly chastened for my stupidity.

At one point we visited a road where most of the houses had been burnt out in a riot early on in 'The Troubles' and left deserted. To rebuild would have been provocative. One end of the street, however, had escaped destruction and was occupied by what was clearly a Roman Catholic community. It was August, the month of Corpus Christi, and a large banner had been slung on high between the houses across the street: the text said it all: 'This is my Body'.

At the conclusion of our reconnaissance visit, we thankfully climbed on to a plane on Aldergrove runway. As we sped down the tarmac, we were paced by an armoured car, as a deterrent to terrorists with heat-seeking missiles.

In due course 40 children duly arrived at Gatwick and were welcomed to our parishioners' homes – the Catholics to Anglican homes and vice versa. The two weeks were a great success. The youngsters met and played together in a way that would not have been possible in Belfast. At the rectory we put up a couple of young boys traumatised by the violence, in which one had lost an uncle. One lad could only with difficulty be enticed by our daughter Helen to come out from under his bed.

The Roman Catholics had brought with them a social worker called Nellie. At the end of the time I asked her how she thought it had gone. "Oh, sure, there's been no trouble at all. Nobody's mentioned religion once!" There was only one hoax call from a young voice with an Irish accent phoning the police to say that a (fortunately imaginary) bomb had been planted in a local school. One thing all the Irish children wanted to see was the sight of an unarmed policeman. The holidays as a whole were joyful and positive times. Perhaps they opened a fresh horizon on a world where two communities could co-exist in peace.

A longer term overseas engagement resulted from my membership of the Salisbury Diocesan Sudan Committee. After the British withdrew from the Sudan in 1956, it was not long before the Muslim government found an excuse to expel foreign missionaries from the south. They left, shaking their heads sadly and bemoaning their premature departure. "It's too soon. The Sudanese Church will never be able to manage on its own." Somewhat to their pique, the reverse proved to be the case. The Sudanese Church, certainly the (Anglican) Episcopal Church of the Sudan (ECS), expanded exponentially, spawning new dioceses on the way. Thus it was that in 1984 there was to be the consecration of not one but of five new bishops in the cathedral of the south's largest city, Juba. A strong link had been formed between the ECS and the Diocese of Salisbury, replacing the now unacceptable partnership with the European missionaries. Salisbury, therefore, had to be represented at this landmark event and it was decided that Askew was the man for the job. With a bit of special pleading, I convinced the committee that Margaret was ideally suited to accompany me. So it was that we both flew out to Khartoum, exactly 25 years after setting up our first home there.

Much had changed. During our previous time in Khartoum, five years into independence, the country looked back with remarkable nostalgia and even gratitude for the years of British rule. In the intervening years Communism had come and gone, to be replaced by a stricter Islamism. Instead of the moral uprightness and hospitality of the previous kinder expression of Islam, now taxi-drivers, for instance, on seeing a European, might bang on their car doors and abusively shout *khawaja* (foreigner). Some of the infrastructure had broken down and not been replaced: electric street-lighting cables, for instance, lay uncovered on the pavements, unprotected by paving slabs. Khartoum was a sadder city than we remembered.

We flew straight on to the south – new territory, closed to us in British Council days, when the Sudan government suspected the Brits of plans to annex the south to Uganda (which would have made good ethnic sense). It was a joyful revelation for us to discover a Sudanese civilisation, not Arab but African, not Muslim but largely Christian. By now, some expatriate missionaries had been allowed back, as guests and technical advisers of the Sudanese Church. Two such expats looked after us and took us about. With them we travelled up country to the theological college, named still after the first British bishop, Bishop Gwynne. Here we found a saintly Sudanese principal, intent on breaking down tribalism in the college and creating a non-segmented Christian community.

Two events resonate from that fascinating journey along dirt tracks to Bishop Gwynne College. One was our stop at a wayside parish church, where the Church Council happened to be in session. They abandoned their agenda with suspicious alacrity and gathered round to greet us. The pastor and his wife chased the chicken off the table, sat us down and offered us traditional Sudanese hospitality for travellers – a glass of water. As we reached out gratefully for the glasses, the pastor stopped us and we paused while he said grace over the water. At once we saw through a chink in the glossy walls of our civilisation into another world where water does not flow on demand from the tap but has to be carried daily in a jerrican on someone's shoulders from a distant well.

The second memorable pause in our journey came at the town of Lui. Here a missionary, Dr Fraser, fresh from Army medical service, arrived with his retinue in 1922. The doctor, his wife and sister travelled on bicycles, while a column of bearers toiled behind with their possessions. The head man was unfamiliar with Europeans, let alone missionary doctors, and was suspicious. Then a woman staggered out of the bush, mauled by a lion, and the doctor asked permission to treat her. Reckoning she would die anyway, the head man agreed. After Dr Fraser's administrations, however, the woman recovered and his value was recognised.

He set to work on three fronts – medical work, education and preaching; his sermons he delivered under a vast tree on the edge of the town, preaching the message of freedom, where only 30 years previously Arab slave-traders had conducted their auctions. The doctor had a particular gift for involving others in his work. At the time of our visit, Lui was still a simple society, where herdsmen took bows and arrows out with them to shoot something for the pot. Three memorials to Dr Fraser's work could be seen – a large secondary school, the provincial hospital, and a vast corrugated iron church presided over by a Sudanese pastor who would have made St Paul look half-hearted. Out of that rural community, I was told, 18 men had been trained up to qualify as doctors.

Back at Juba, the consecration duly took place amid great celebrations. It was a joyful and heart-warming event, and we were made most welcome. In due course, we returned to Khartoum en route for home. Part of my task had been to take photos and record singing for a tape/slide presentation to travel the Salisbury Diocese on my return. This, as it turned out, was not to be my last visit to the Sudan. For Margaret and myself there has remained a permanent Sudanese dimension to our ministry and our affections.

Another precious African experience came about through visiting our son Peter in Ethiopia during part of his gap year. Here he was assisting my former colleague, Charles Sherlock, who was assistant chaplain at the Anglican Chaplaincy in Addis Ababa. It was not long after the disastrous famine, which, with the efforts of Bob Geldof, had caught the world's attention and compassion. Money had been sent out to the chaplaincy and with it they set up a home, with government help, for the many orphans. This work had expanded to four homes. During our time in this beautiful but drought-stricken country we visited with Peter the most recently established home, on a cold upland plateau. This prompted Margaret to set up a project to make warm tracksuits for the full total of 600 orphans. As mentioned in Chapter 11, this she achieved with the help of the Mothers'

Union and craft contacts across the diocese. Working parties met daily in the cellar, which had not seen so much activity since the Middle Ages. Eventually, after a couple of months, Margaret stumbled up, mole-like, from the depths, feeling her way in the unaccustomed sunshine. We watched as our other son, Christopher, drove off in a hired van, loaded to the roof with beautiful multi-coloured tracksuits, to Southampton docks. The commitment of the helpers and the generosity of wholesalers in supplying free materials had been immense.

Tracksuits in the making

A further Developing World visit awaited us when we moved to Bath Abbey and the Bath and Wells Diocese. Here the diocesan link was with Zambia and Bath Abbey established a special relationship with the Zambian seminary at Kitwe. Once again, the two of us were despatched on a special mission to cement the link. The problems of Zambia did not appear quite so crushing as those that oppressed the southern Sudan, where decades of civil war had paralysed development. However, even in our short stay in Zambia, we observed the terrible inroads caused by Aids and the poverty resulting from the decline in the copper mining industry. On one occasion we were taken to what we were told was "the largest hole in the world": it was a vast cavity on the earth's surface that had once been the scene of open-cast copper mining. Now, the copper exhausted, it was a sad sight, though the surrounding huts, once populated by the workforce, were still inhabited. We were taken to one such home where a pathetic sight confronted us: the hut belonged to the parents of a young woman who had married a curate newly trained at the seminary. Tragically, he had died of Aids and the family had gathered with the girl to grieve with her. Silently, we squatted down to join the group and sat in silence for some time with them: words were not required, just some empathy into bright hopes extinguished.

The seminary formed part of an impressive educational campus. It had had a rocky history but was now in the secure hands of a vigorous Sudanese expat, John Kanyikwa, whom we had known when he had been Provincial Secretary in Juba. He and his wife, Lilian, received us warmly and put us up for our stay. He was keen to build manual and self-supporting work into the college curriculum and to this end Bath Abbey had already given cash to set up a chicken farm, producing eggs not only for the college but to sell at market: this was flourishing. Now we wanted to move on to establish banana trees on the same basis. You can imagine our joy, a year after our return, when we received from the seminary a video of the graduation day. Above the ranks of students in their very best clothes, and the marquees erected for the occasion, we could see the upper branches of massive banana palms.

Our visit to the seminary was a happy time; Margaret taught useful crafts to the wives: showing how to convert an ordinary shirt into a 'clerical', to accommodate a 'dog-collar', and making church candles, using empty plastic containers as moulds. She had brought with her a suitcase full of little bags of wax in powder form. It was only when we reached the Zambian customs office that we realised that our bags of powder looked suspiciously like illegal drugs. Fortunately, we appeared innocent enough to be believed. At the college I lectured about church life in Britain. The week culminated in a dance, the first ever held in the college.

We had already benefited from our older son's gap year – an institution now regarded as a basic human right by most school-leavers. Our friend Alastair Whitelaw, teaching at King's College, Auckland, had invited Chris to visit New Zealand and work as an assistant master at the school. He needed no parental encouragement to go and we were invited to pay him a visit. We agreed gratefully, asking only for some preaching while there to justify my existence. We cherish warm memories of lush scenery and open-handed hospitality.

This recital of our overseas links would not be complete without reference to Brunswick. In 1942 Bath sustained two nights of heavy bombing in one of the "Baedeker raids", in retaliation for the Allied bombing of Lubeck. Over the two nights 400 people died and they are buried in a mass grave in the city cemetery. To mark the 50th anniversary of this tragic event, the City Council decided to invite representatives of the City Council of our twinned city of Brunswick (Braunschweig). There were to be two services – a simple memorial service in the morning at the cemetery, where lay the mass grave: this service our German guests would not attend. Then there was to be an afternoon civic service at the Abbey. I decided that if the morning's theme was to be commemoration, then the afternoon should focus on reconciliation. To my surprise, this caused much alarm among the City Council at the Guildhall, where the war was thought to be much too recent for such an audacious venture. I dug my toes in and said that if the City fathers did not like the thought of reconciliation they would have to find another church (I knew full well that no other church in Bath could accommodate them). In the event, all went well and we hosted the service: my colleague Charles Stewart delivered a lengthy welcome in German; the two mayors shook hands. Our mayor was in tears by the end. Nobody complained.

From this sprang a significant sequel. In 1944 Brunswick had suffered a far more serious raid by the RAF's 1,000 bomber fleet and 4,000 died – 10 times the Bath death toll. Many of them were slave workers, who were not allowed into the bunkers built to protect the citizens of Braunschweig. I found myself invited to preach at their commemorative service. This had been planned by a Lutheran pastor, the "Dom Prediger" of the cathedral, Joachim Hempel. Born in Brunswick, he had grown up in the ruins of the city. He was using the anniversary to fill in the gaps in the German history books, so a month-long course of lectures explored the role of the Gestapo in Braunschweig, the fate of the Jewish community and so on. The events were planned on the grand scale. The service in the cathedral was timed for the moment of the RAF's arrival – 2.00am. It was preceded by a service in the Roman Catholic cathedral, where columns of people from all over the city converged, described their route – past the ruins of the synagogue, for instance – and read a prayer. My task in preaching at the Lutheran service was not easy. What can one say? I must have been given some of the right words because afterwards I was hugged by a Lutheran bishop!

Thus began a fruitful exchange of visits and we made some good friends among the congregation of Joachim's church. On one occasion we were taken to see the Town Hall as guests of the friendly mayor. Unfortunately, he had no more English than I had German: in my days at school learning German was thought to be an unpatriotic activity and the language had not been taught. I noticed on the wall an in *memoriam* plaque from the war: as I read it I realised that, while most had died fighting for their country, there were others remembered here who had been executed by the regime.

Joachim subsequently preached at our VE Day commemoration. The Abbey was packed with rows of the British Legion, many of them most unhappy at having a German preacher on that occasion above all. Joachim turned them round in two minutes in words which recalled the German Churches' statement in 1945: "This was all our fault: it was we Germans who brought all this misery on Europe". At the end of the service he planted an apple tree of peace outside the Abbey to loud applause "The leaves of the tree are for the healing of the nations." (Colour picture)

So concludes this list of "foreign affairs" – with one exception – our pilgrimages, which deserve a separate chapter to themselves.

Chapter 15

TO BE A PILGRIM

WHAN that Aprille with his shoures soote
The droghte of Marche hath perced to the roote,
And specially, from every shires ende
Of Engelond, to Caunterbury they wende,
The holy blisful martir for to seke,
That hem hath holpen, whan that they were seke.

So begins the first masterpiece composed in the English language, Chaucer's *Canterbury Tales*, recounting the stories told by that band of pilgrims on the road to Canterbury.

Pilgrimage is embedded in the heart of most great religions. In Islam it is the life aim of Muslims to get to Mecca once in their lifetime. Orthodox Jews have similar feelings about reaching the land of Israel. The mass gathering of Hindus by the banks of the Ganges some years ago produced the world's biggest ever crowd, visible from space. And from the very early days Christians have flocked to the sites associated with the life of Jesus and, to a lesser extent, the lives of the saints.

It had always been an ambition of mine to travel at some point to Palestine and my time at Salisbury Cathedral provided the opportunity. So it was that in 1988 I signed up with Inter-Church Travel to go on a week-long course in Israel for potential pilgrimage leaders. It was just after Christmas and the weather was miserable (it rained every day and on one day it snowed) but after that week I was hooked. On my return I sold

Via Dolorosa

the idea to a deeply wary Margaret and the next year we gathered our first pilgrimage group, mainly from the cathedral congregation. With the help of Inter-Church, we set off first to Galilee, then up to Jerusalem. It proved effective beyond our wildest dreams. Cathedrals often attract large congregations but these tend to be anonymous and even a little impersonal: indeed, some people choose cathedral worship because they want to keep a low profile and avoid the commitment that builds up within a smaller group. A pilgrimage, on the other hand, is an intense experience of Christian community and the impact of this was very powerful on a random group recruited *ad hoc* to spend 12 days together.

Margaret and I were both surprised and gratified by this unexpected result of our planning. A sequel was required, so we sketched out a journey pursuing St Paul round the Turkish coast, across to Greece and to Athens. And that was the beginning of a series of horizon-widening trips, following first St Paul, then discovering the Seven Churches of the Book of Revelation and, later, opening up the great days of the early Church in Cappadocia and across Jordan and Syria. Italy was soon added to the bundle, with visits to Assisi and Rome.

We were with St Paul as he said farewell to the elders of Ephesus on the shore at Miletus (a moment so moving that it reduced our lesson-reader, a judge, to tears). We sat beneath the Syrian pillar from which Simeon had preached to the pilgrim masses who had toiled even from distant Britannia to listen to him. We created a riot in the theatre at Ephesus, clamouring the praises of Diana of the Ephesians to the great amusement of a group of Americans, unused to the sight of an Anglican riot. We stood outside the Bishop's Palace in Assisi, imagining the good bishop's embarrassment as Francis stripped off his fine clothes and threw them at his father's feet. And we sat, profoundly moved, beside the ancient roadway from the Kedron Valley to the High Priest's house, the very track up which Jesus must have been dragged in that first Holy Week. Such moments embodied for us what we came to recognise as "the tingle factor".

Always the main thread of our time together was provided by links with the Bible or early Church history, imaginatively entering into the last week of Jesus's life on earth; or empathising with Peter or Paul; or Constantine; or Justinian and his remarkable wife Theodora. We clutched at every opportunity to let history leap into life. Margaret, her first suspicions dispelled, found a real vocation in this task; she brought to vivid existence one of the 'dead cities' near Aleppo, Sejilla, deserted by Byzantine Christians, probably because of plague. As we walked round the ruins, carefully primed and costumed pilgrims popped out of the buildings to explain who they were: Irene waxed eloquent about the bath house mosaics and Julia, *grande dame* of the village, told us about her stately home. All this proved to be such good entertainment that guides with other groups were clamouring for copies of the script.

Our pilgrimages were billed as 'holidays with a Christian purpose' and we stuck to this theme of learning and discovery. Every day contained worship – perhaps an opening prayer on the coach, then a set piece address with hymns on some rocky hillside, and finally night prayer back at the hotel. The addresses, typed up in advance and photocopied, gave everyone a record of the themes. Margaret produced elegant daily A5 sheets, known as Margaret's Memos, containing information about the day's programme and appropriate prayer. This obviated the need for frequent verbal notices. We shared the work of leadership with one or two others, depending on the size of the group, and on one occasion Margaret's brother, John, stepped in at the last moment when I was unable to go. It was a great leap forward when we moved from Inter-Church to the more specialised pilgrimage firm of McCabe's, who gave us excellent and knowledgeable service.

All this might sound both activist and earnest but we had a great deal of fun as well. Visiting a newly renovated restaurant in Nablus, Margaret complimented the *maitre d'* on his achievement. He, feeling something was required in return, replied: "And you, madam, are nearly quite beautiful." This comment was well received by our coach load of pilgrims when we passed it on to them.

Then there was the occasion in the Church of the Holy Sepulchre in Jerusalem when the thronging crowds seemed even more diverse and exotic than usual. On the left, a procession of Latin (ie Roman Catholic) Franciscans was heading off to mass, while another line of deeply bearded Orthodox priests, led by Muslim vergers in fezzes, came the other way. A noisy gaggle of Catholic Mothers of Milwaukee vied with some equally raucous Italian ladies by the steps to Calvary. Queuing to enter the Aedicule, which commemorates Jesus's tomb, I gazed at this alien spectacle, and then remarked – I thought *sotto voce* – to my churchwarden next to me in the queue: "What a comfort it is to know that God is really an Anglican". At this, an American lady in front of us spun round and whispered fiercely: "How do you know She is?"

Quite apart from the grand buildings and the big experiences, some of our best moments have been the simple meeting of individuals across the cultural chasms that separate us. On our last visit to Petra, my friend Louis van den Berg and I left the seething crowds on the valley floor and climbed up the steep hillside to a place of barren rocks and sheer cliffs. Turning a corner we came on a lean-to structure up against the rock face. Inside at the back, seated in the corner, we could see an elderly black-clad Bedouin lady. I marshalled my Arabic to wish her "Salaam". In reply she simply looked at us and enquired – "Cuppatea?" The invitation was irresistible and we spent a rich half hour with her and her family. One grandson spoke some English and told us that his granny lived in a cave – "but a three star cave".

Some of the deepest moments were times of worship in unusual settings – the prayers while seated on the edge of a Turkish trench in Gallipoli, with our Turkish guide reading the words of remembrance; the celebration of Holy Communion at the open-air altar in Galilee, with the water lapping on the shore in the background. (Colour picture) Latterly, a great bonus was to discover kindred spirits in Barney and Esme Hopkinson, who co-led half a dozen expeditions with us. Barney had been our archdeacon in Salisbury Diocese and Esme was a trained nurse. I treasure a memory of Barney celebrating Holy Communion on a Greek hillside so steep that he needed a deacon permanently kneeling in front of him to hold up the elements!

Our 20th pilgrimage – to Israel/Palestine – was a happy and inspiring time, confirming our faith in the power of pilgrimage. Over the years many relatives and friends have joined us to discover for themselves the pilgim experience and we were particularly pleased that both John Liversedge, my Best Man in 1959, and his brother Dick were able to be with us. This was something of a comfort when, just before Christmas in the same year, John died suddenly. We said farewell to a good friend of longstanding and we thank God for the time he had been able to share with his brother on that pilgrimage.

A particularly happy and significant pilgrimage to Israel/Palestine in 2013 marked the end of our travels with Barney and Esme. After this we continued with further invaluable help from our good friends Selina Deacon and Diana Tear. Margaret and I had notched up a total of 23 pilgrimages over the years.

Our final journey was once more to Turkey, accompanied to our great joy by very many friends who had travelled with us before. The notion of pilgrimage forms a valuable picture both for the life of the Church and also for the lifetime of each pilgrim. For the Church, it symbolises a dynamic picture of people on the move at their own pace, not just a static image of sheep in a sheep-pen. For the individual, it suggests our journey through the different stages of life towards Jesus, who is both our destination and our companion along the road.

Chapter 16

RETIRING – BUT IN STAGES

After leaving Bath Abbey (my departure being precipitously hastened by the health problems already described), we moved into the house awaiting us in Crockerton, just south of Warminster. Our move happened not long after Easter, so it seemed appropriate to change the cottage's name from Fir Tree Cottage to Easter Cottage. This was to mark not only the season but also the seemingly miraculous recovery I had been given the previous year through the wonders of cardiac surgery.

Of course, during all these preceding years the Askew clan had been growing, with sons- and daughters-in-law welcomed into the family. In time, too, came further joy with the births of 13 grandchildren, each one unique and treasured. We relished our new home, full of character and possibilities, and all the family enjoyed the rural delights of meadow, forest and lake on the doorstep. With the help of a builder neighbour we were able to reconstruct one side of the house to make it ideal for bed and breakfast, while the lodge in the garden was already suitable for holiday lets. This enabled us to pay the mortgage and balance the books – just! Nevertheless, when a vacancy in the Warminster clergy team came up a year after we moved in, it seemed right to apply for the post, at least for the next three year period. So, in the summer of 2011, I found myself team vicar of the Cley Hill (Warminster) team, with responsibility for three churches in the Deverill Valley and a further three grouped round Corsley, on the other side of the Longleat Estate.

Given three years to look after six churches, what was I to do? Just to keep the show on the road seemed unimaginative. Three years was not long enough to develop an in-depth pastoral ministry – the dear old vicar peddling down the valley, hailing every parishioner by name! So – what to do?

A few years earlier at the Abbey we had, somewhat heart in mouth, embarked on the well-known course of lay training called The Alpha Course. It was based on the rectory, where Margaret heroically undertook to lead a team in providing 60 people with a meal each week for 10 weeks. For our spiritual food, the Alpha recipe was simple – a shared meal, a talk on some aspect of basic Christianity, and a final half hour of lay-led discussion groups from which the clergy were rigidly excluded. In Bath it had worked well and provided an excellent stimulus and wake-up call to a previously somewhat torpid congregation. But would it work out in the country? There was only one way to find out.

Corsley, the largest of the villages on the Bath side of Longleat, is remarkable for its lack of a centre: it is 30 miles of lanes connecting minor hamlets. We had two assets – a good hall and a good man to head the course up: Richard Dean, a retired naval commander, was the ideal kingpin. Greatly daring, we defied the maxim about there being no such thing as a free dinner and invited the entire community to a free dinner and 'taster' evening. Seventy people attended and most stuck with us for the succeeding weeks.

This simple structure and old-fashioned 'chalk and talk' teaching method had dramatic results. Two of the discussion group leaders discovered a calling to ordination through the experience and in due course they donned their dog-collars to be NSM (Non-stipendiary Ministers). This proved to be of crucial importance for the future of ministry in the parish. A second

137

Alpha course, in the Deverill Valley, held in the local pub, was also well attended and fruitful, while not yielding the spectacular outcome we had seen in Corsley.

The remainder of my time was spent in the usual parish duties, known vulgarly as 'hatching, matching and dispatching', which are actually opportunities to be with people at the most critical points in their lives. These tasks had their lighter moments. There was, for example, the burial of a gentleman in his 80s who had grown up in the valley: the service was attended by the 84 grandchildren presented to him by his 16 sons and daughters. When I ventured to ask the undertaker if people had heard of birth control in the Deverill Valley, he reminded me there had been nothing much else to do before the coming of television.

Engagement with Crockerton's Church School was fun. With the head teacher as my ally, I was able to promote a donkey-led procession along the half mile to the village pub, to discover if there was any room in the inn. Probably Health and Safety regulations would not allow it these days but it did provide an indelible live nativity scene for a generation of children.

It was the congregations of these two parishes that made my time as team vicar so enjoyable. A backbone of ex-Services people and farmers ensured that plenty happened and that events were well run. It was with considerable regret that I came to the end of my three years and said farewell to full-time church ministry. At my retirement party Margaret referred firmly to my "retiring for the second and final time". I got the message.

Those three years, pretending to be a country vicar for the first time in my career provided a happy and surprisingly satisfying conclusion to my formal, full-time ministry.

Now that the diocese was no longer paying our mortgage as part of my stipend, some downsizing became imperative. The sale of Easter Cottage made possible the purchase of a delightful bungalow two villages up the valley. In due course, after three years, the size of the garden became oppressive and a further move brought us to Westwood, just outside Bradford-on-Avon.

At this point, a new concern began to engage us. Richard Dean, our Corsley friend, had always been a strong supporter of the diocesan link with the Episcopal Church of the Sudan. Together with other members of our diocesan Sudan Committee, he visited Juba, the principal city of the southern Sudan, with a population of 800,000. In a conversation the Sudanese archbishop, himself a former headmaster, described the sad state of education, ruined by decades of civil war: could Salisbury Diocese help with the building of a new secondary school in Juba? The Episcopal Church, running 10 primary schools in Juba, would welcome a secondary school to receive the children for the next stage of their education. As illiteracy was running at 85 per cent, this was clearly a vital need.

Within a couple of years Richard had brought about the building and opening of Juba Diocesan Model Secondary School. With the help of great generosity from a Salisbury church, the British government and a number of individuals, the school opened its doors to 96 students in 2007, rising year on year to near 700. (Colour picture) Richard asked Margaret and myself to join the committee in Salisbury supporting the venture. Margaret rapidly became the Sponsorship Administrator, presiding over the links that enabled 115 students to be individually sponsored with a bursary. I had the less dramatic portfolio of writing to trusts and charities to ask for money for our various capital projects. To help me see the needs more clearly, in 2010 I went out to south Sudan, primarily to take photos for a DVD of the school, to be used for promotional purposes. Students lead a daily school assembly and pack the mid-week Christian Union. To see the school growing and flourishing despite various difficulties and disappointments has been a spiritual encouragement for us all on the Support Group.

Retirement can appear to be a dark shadow over the future but the secret, it seems to me, is wherever possible to have something to retire to, as well as a life's work to retire from. Given health and strength, retirement can be a widening of opportunities and an enhancement of life.

The last word

Growing older would be so much simpler if one grew older inside, so that one felt one's age. I don't. I still recognise warmly the timid youngster who in the words of a school song *went off to Harrow, tra-la-la/ and was placed in the lower, Lower Third*; or the would-be warrior who marched up the road in which we lived in East Grinstead to catch the train that would eventually take him via Wales to Army service in Egypt; or the thwarted film-goer who exchanged a 3 shilling and 6 pence seat in the stalls for a crowded rear pew seat to hear Billy Graham; or the young man who drove across country from East Grinstead, accompanied by his Best Man, to be married to Margaret in the little church at Hayes in Kent. Memories crowd in, both deep and wide, stretching from the uplands of Ethiopia to the parkland of the Virginia Seminary outside Washington DC. What does it all add up to? Have I been on a purposeful journey or an aimless meander?

As I try to marshal my recollections into line to see if they form a coherent pathway, I am first of all conscious of a massive debt of gratitude. I think first of Margaret, my amazing omni-competent companion of 56 years – what would my life have been without her? Next to her in the front rank are spread out our wonderful family and grandchildren, each of them very special people with their gifts, talents and values. Then I cast a sideways glance at the varied selection of houses we've been entrusted with, from that mud-walled, water-soluble bungalow on the edge of Khartoum to the 13th century elegance of our house in Salisbury Close.

Then inevitably my gaze switches to the all-consuming career which has held me gripped for 60 years. Through my life in the ordained ministry, I have been privileged to meet so many hundreds of people in situations that range from the heartbreaking to the hilarious. The Christian family in all its manifestations has become 'home' for me, resolving my early anxieties about where I fitted in and belonged. Having done my best initially to avoid entry into the priesthood, as I look back now I feel shame about my initial reluctance, and, once within it, about the individuals I have failed: but I am also grateful for a life that has stretched me and been deeply fulfilling. Many of my theological landmarks have changed over the years but if I am left with rather fewer passionate convictions, those that remain might perhaps glow more brightly and be even more deeply held. Of these the most central is, of course, that Christ was and is unique, expressing God through a human personality, opening a way through to the Father for us, humbling Himself to be our companion and brother, to death and beyond.

Inevitably, as one gets older, one looks forward to the journey's end as well as backwards at the ground traversed. (Colour picture) Here, the Christian faith offers us a 'blessed hope', in which I am content to rest. Of course, it is impossible to imagine what the future holds but I take heart from John's agnosticism (1 John 3:2): "Here and now, dear friends, we are God's children. What we shall be has not yet been disclosed. When it is disclosed, we shall be like Christ; for we shall see Him as He is."

In *Pilgrim's Progress*, Christian and his companion reach a vast upland plateau as they near the Celestial City. They are encouraged by some shepherds, who lend them a 'perspective glass' through which they glimpse the gates of the city "and some of the glory of the place". I am deeply grateful that I too have been given at least a glimpse of that glory.

Acknowledgements

These memoirs had their origins in a hospital bed in the Royal United Hospital, Bath.

I occupied the bed briefly in 1999 and each day our son Peter, who lived nearby, on his return from London at about 10pm, would bring in to me the chapter his wife, Fiona, had typed up during the day. Given this flying start it would have been churlish to leave the text incomplete, so over time the opportunity was found to finish the job.

From then on many people have helped. My wife, Margaret, and niece Elizabeth Johnson polished off the rest of the typing, while Edward (Liz's husband), a skilled photographer, took the front cover photograph and helped greatly with the other illustrations.

Lord Carey, my former diocesan bishop, in the middle of a hectic summer, was good enough to write the foreword. Next, the text was passed to Margaret's brother, the Rev John Peirce, himself a published author, who skilfully co-ordinated its onward progress with his editor and printer.

To all the team I am deeply grateful, particularly to Margaret. Behind her stand our children and grandchildren, our distraction, diversion and delight, whose story this is too.

RICHARD ASKEW

Richard Askew's previous book "One Man's Bath" may be obtained direct from him, email rgaskew@gmail.com (Price £7)